THE POET
THE BARONESS

THE POET
THE BARONESS

W.H. Auden and Stella Musulin, a Friendship

Michael O'Sullivan

 CEU PRESS

CENTRAL EUROPEAN UNIVERSITY PRESS
BUDAPEST–VIENNA–NEW YORK

Published in 2023 by
CENTRAL EUROPEAN UNIVERSITY PRESS

Nádor utca 9, H-1051 Budapest, Hungary
Tel: +36-1-327-3138 or 327-3000
E-mail: *ceupress@press.ceu.edu*
Website: *www.ceupress.com*

ISBN 978-963-386-655-9 (paperback)
ISBN 978-963-386-656-6 (ebook)

Library of Congress Cataloging-in-Publication Data

Names: O'Sullivan, Michael, 1957- author.
Title: The poet & the baroness : W.H. Auden and Stella Musulin, a friendship / Michael O'Sullivan.
Other titles: The poet and the baroness
Description: Budapest ; New York : Central European University Press, 2023. | Includes index.
Identifiers: LCCN 2023038685 (print) | LCCN 2023038686 (ebook) | ISBN 9789633866559 (paperback) | ISBN 9789633866566 (pdf)
Subjects: LCSH: Auden, W. H. (Wystan Hugh), 1907-1973--Friends and associates. | Authors, English--20th century--Biography. | Musulin, Stella--Friends and associates. | Friendship--Austria--Vienna--History--20th century. | BISAC: BIOGRAPHY & AUTOBIOGRAPHY / Literary Figures | LCGFT: Biographies.
Classification: LCC PR6001.U4 Z7646 2023 (print) | LCC PR6001.U4 (ebook) | DDC 821/.912 [B]--dc23/eng/20230825
LC record available at https://lccn.loc.gov/2023038685
LC ebook record available at https://lccn.loc.gov/2023038686

Contents

For Marko, Christopher, and Caroline Musulin

Acknowledgments

My principal debt of gratitude is to Marko Musulin, Stella's son, for his memories of his mother, for allowing me to reproduce her journals and family photographs, and for reading the manuscript. Professor Edward Mendelson, Auden's literary executor, kindly gave me permission to reproduce Auden's letters to Stella and encouraged the project ab initio. Dr Philip Mansel and Richard Bassett shared their memories of Stella. Bryony Bethell read the manuscript, and I am immensely grateful to her for her useful suggestions and improvements to the text. Thomas Sneddon provided invaluable assistance in the final stages of the book's production. Timo Fruwirth of the project for the digitalisation of the Auden/Musulin papers gave me early access to the invaluable help this worthy enterprise provides for Auden scholars. The project, under the skilful direction of Dr. Sandra Mayer, will be an ongoing source for scholars interested in the period of Auden's time as a resident of Austria. Zeynep, John, and Freya Ostromouff gave me their unique and special support in Somerset as did Maura Dillon-Malone. I wish to remember two dear friends who have died; Peter Müller, founder of the International Auden Society, who first introduced me to Stella forty years ago, and Paul O'Grady, historian of English Catholicism with whom I spent many happy hours in Vienna in the 1980s discussing various aspects of Auden's life and work. Kristian Kolar of the University of Maribor kindly gave me access to his detailed research on the Serbian roots of the Musulin family. Ricarda Denzer and Professor Monika Seidl have permitted me to quote extracts from my contribution to their 2014 project *Silence Turned into Objects: W.H. Auden in Kirchstetten*. Finally, I thank my editors at CEU Press, Linda Kunos and Emily Poznanski, for their stalwart support. I am especially grateful to John Puckett for his excellent editorial input.

"Not everything about Wystan Auden was very appetising, his private life was a mess. But he was kind, generous and unpretentious, and personally, I was devoted to him. [He was] an amazing mixture of talent, high scholarship, wretchedness and squalor."

From Stella Musulin's journals

Discovering Auden:
A Personal Journey

W.H. Auden has become so central to my life over the past forty years that there never appears to have been a time that it could have been otherwise. He is, for me, a talismanic touchstone. My conversation has become so peppered with quotes from his work and about his life that I am frequently asked when I first met him. I was still at school in Ireland when he died in 1973. His niece married an Irishman, and the poet's great-niece was at Trinity College Dublin with me. However, Auden, the great peregrinus, a visitor to nearly thirty countries, never set foot in Ireland.

My English teacher and mentor, T.F. Lane, first made me aware that Yeats and not Ireland featured more in Auden's poetry. "Ireland has her madness and her weather still" is the nearest we come to an Audenesque Hiberno travelogue. He enjoyed telling how immensely proud he was of writing a poem in a complex Gaelic meter. He also demonstrated an extraordinary knowledge of contemporary Irish politics when he came to write "The Public v. The Late Mr W.B. Yeats" in 1939. It was a time when he was beginning to question the influence of Yeats on his work and to consider also, Yeats's politics which he found distasteful.

Auden significantly influenced modern Irish poets, including Patrick Kavanagh, Seamus Heaney, and Derek Mahon. In *Finnegans Wake*, he appears as a terse footnote in which Joyce acknowledged the young poet's claim to Nordic ancestry when he wrote, "I bolt that thor. Auden." He read *Finnegans Wake* soon after its publication and, like Evelyn Waugh, was not especially taken by it. However, it did have a limited influence on aspects of "The Age of Anxiety." In an interview with *The Paris Review*, he offered this view on the work: "Obviously, he's a great genius—but his work is simply too long. Joyce said that he wanted people to spend their life on his work. For me, life is too short and too precious. I feel the same way about *Ulysses*. Also, *Finnegans Wake* can't be read the way one reads ordinarily." He had a brief youthful flirtation with the mystical verse of Yeats's friend George Russell (Æ), and he brilliantly described Oscar Wilde as "a phoney prophet but a serious playboy." *The Ascent of F6* was produced at Dublin's innovative Gate Theatre in 1939. There, with those flimsy associations, the possibility of any more substantial links between Auden and Ireland ends.

My own connection to Auden and his world began at Trinity when I chose him as the subject of my postgraduate work in the English Department. Charles Osborne's biography of Auden had just been published and serialised in *The Observer*. I recall reading the first extract in *The Observer* on a wet Irish Sunday in March 1980. I was fascinated by the details of a life which were largely unknown to me and many others, and I found them an absolute revelation, if not indeed something of a sensation. However, that book was soon to be eclipsed by the biography Humphrey Carpenter was about to publish.

"Burn my letters," Auden exhorted his friends by appealing to his estate to publish press notices with this request after his death. His literary executors did as they were requested.

Fortunately, few of his friends acquiesced to his wish, and most of those who Humphrey Carpenter contacted gave him access to their correspondence with Auden.

Throughout his life, he railed on about his abhorrence of the idea of someone writing his biography. "A writer is a maker, not a man of action" was the oft-repeated mantra. He claimed that reading a man's personal letters after his death was as impertinent as reading them while he lived. As in so much else, he was a mass of contradictions. While waiting in his tutor's rooms at Oxford, he casually picked up letters from his desk and began reading them. When his newly appointed tutor, Nevill Coghill, arrived, Auden told him a page from a particular letter was missing and asked him where it might be found. So, while not wishing other people to be tourists in his life, Auden had no difficulty making occasional visits to the lives of others.

A letter from me to Humphrey Carpenter brought a most courteous, if slightly guarded, reply. I had been given a research award to look at Auden's papers and related material at Oxford and thought it a good idea to contact his biographer, who lived in the city. We arranged to meet at a public house much frequented by Oxford students. After a few ice-breaking drinks, my youthful enthusiasm for Auden struck a chord with Humphrey, and he invited me home to lunch with his wife and family. Only after much convivial banter did I realise, to my absolute surprise, that the real purpose of the invitation was to show me the vast quantity of material he had amassed during the course of his research for the Auden biography.

To my even greater surprise, when I was leaving, he handed me a large box containing much of that material, saying, "This should help you with your research." I then moved through a sweltering Oxford with this weighty gift, quietly in awe of my generous benefactor and thinking how lucky Auden was to have had such a man as the chronicler of his life. It was the beginning of one of many friendships initiated through my burgeoning Auden obsession and which brought me into the direct path of many of his friends.

An old friendship and some new ones also brought me to Austria and towards a more tangible connection to Auden's Austrian life. In 1982 an Irish scholar and writer, Patrick Healy, introduced me to the American artist Timothy Hennessy, who was organising a major exhibition of his work in Paris as a tribute to James Joyce. It was part of the centenary celebrations of Joyce's birth. A central part of that exhibition was Patrick Healy's reading of the complete text of *Finnegans Wake*. On the sidelines of that event, I met the then Vienna-based linguist and translator Lise Rosenbaum. She told me of the existence in Vienna of The International Auden Society, founded by Peter Müller of the Bundesdenkmalamt and the author and journalist Karlheinz Roschitz.

A letter to Peter Müller brought a reply inviting me to stay with him in Vienna. Within a week of arriving, the idea of an exhibition and symposium to mark the 10th anniversary of Auden's death, which fell the next year, was born. Müller was an extraordinary man, and though he travelled extensively in the rarefied world of both the Austrian intellectual and aristocratic set, he never lost touch with his roots in a small village in Lower Austria. He possessed a charm and self-assurance which left him equally at ease in a castle or cottage. I remember him bringing me to see the blood-stained uniform of the murdered Archduke Franz Ferdinand when this relic of Sarajevo was being inspected by his office. For a moment, we were alone with the glass lid lifted. We looked at each other and at the uniform, and then he suddenly said, "Go on, touch it, touch all that terrible history." I declined his offer. He brought me on

Stella in the 1940s

many a pilgrimage to places and people associated with Auden's Austrian life. As Auden was just ten years dead, many people in Austria remembered him, and Peter Müller knew all of them.

But none would have as much influence on me personally or on my understanding of W.H. Auden as his friend, an exceptionally intelligent woman, Stella Musulin. She was born Stella Lloyd-Philipps to an old landed gentry family in Dale Castle in Pembrokeshire. Her marriage into the Austrian aristocracy brought the moniker Baroness Stella Musulin de Gomirje. However, she wrote extensively, cleverly, and with piercing insight on a polyglottal range of subjects as plain Stella Musulin.

Austria, Auden's final resting place, his adopted homeland, and arguably where he was happiest during his lifetime, continues to be the country where he is most honoured. In honouring Auden's memory, I came to enjoy my first meaningful role in the Audenworld, which, happily and fortuitously, brought me into contact with some of his closest friends, especially Stella.

Peter Müller was the catalyst in those years for all things celebratory in relation to Auden in Austria. It was while staying with him at his flat in the Schlosselgasse in Vienna in 1983, a moment which I can only best describe as high "camparama," that Müller's notion arose that I should organise an exhibition and symposium to mark the 10th anniversary of Auden's death, which fell in September of that year. He was showing me a crystal wine flagon and glasses from his collection, which were once part of a suite made for Empress Maria Theresa, and at that moment, he said, "Let's fill these up with wine and toast the idea of the Auden exhibition." I like to think that such high camp style would have amused Auden, who was not averse to the odd incursion into the world of high camp himself.

Once the heady intoxication of the wine from Maria Theresa's wine accoutrements had worn off the next day, I was faced with the reality of honouring a commitment to Peter Müller—who took such matters most seriously—to give Vienna the most significant ever public celebration of Auden's life and work. Vienna was accustomed to hosting impressive arts events, and I soon realised that what was expected was something grand. Within a week, Müller had arranged a meeting with the director of the Lower Austrian Society for Art and Culture, Dr. Eugen Scherer. This organisation was the cultural arm of the Lower Austrian government, and they had under their control one of Vienna's premier public art spaces, a gallery in the Künstlerhaus, which was near some of Vienna's major cultural icons—the Konzerthaus, the Musikverein, the Secession, and the State Opera House. Eugen Scherer was immediately taken by the idea and almost instantly guaranteed the not-inconsiderable funding it would take to assemble the celebration of Auden on the scale that we now had in mind.

The catalogue of the Vienna Auden exhibition

In principle, we all agreed that the event could not be a dry academic affair, and it would have to be attractive to a wide parish, not just to Auden enthusiasts. A strong visual element was essential; there would be music, film, commissioned artworks, audio works, and, of course, the Auden texts in their many varied forms. In tandem with all this, it was agreed that a symposium of Auden scholars would deliver a day of papers in the gallery, and from that, a book of essays was published.

Looking at the scale of what was involved, it was also agreed that the event would not happen until 1984, thereby missing the actual date of the 10th anniversary of Auden's death by a few months. But what emerged as the process of organising the event went ahead was the massive global goodwill there was towards Auden and the way in which a veritable cornucopia of the world's most important literary and artistic institutions was willing to weigh in behind an unknown but enthusiastic young scholar from Trinity College Dublin in the most trusting and helpful manner. The catalogue's acknowledgements accompanying the event are a "Who's Who" of that world.

As always with such events, the cast of personalities which emerged lent itself to some great anecdotal lore; as the event got underway, Vienna played host to many of them. Stephen Spender arrived from London along with Auden's biographer Humphrey Carpenter. They were billeted at The Bristol Hotel—then a rather grand but elegantly chipped and faded establishment. At this time, Spender was Poet Laureate and sported a knighthood, under which moniker he was registered at the hotel. It caused hilarious moments at the reception desk where he was always addressed as "Sir Spender," making him sound like something altogether different to any passing English speaker. Chaperoning him around Vienna was a delightful task. He knew the city quite well having lived there in the 1930s. 1984 was the time of the coal miners' strike in England; news of its progress was his abiding obsession. In those pre-internet days, we did our best to keep him updated.

Raymond Adlam of the British Council in Vienna—a man of immense charm and erudition, a much-travelled Council officer and straight from the pages of an Olivia Manning novel—did much to keep the ever-increasing group of distinguished guests entertained. We organised a dinner for Spender in Auden's favourite Vienna restaurant, the Ilona Stüberl, an unpretentious Hungarian bistro on Bräunerstrasse in the inner city, which Auden liked because it had something of pre-1956 Budapest about it. The young artist Mary P. O'Connor who was chosen to illustrate elements of the exhibition was among the guests. She was, at the time working, with Eduardo Paolozzi. Her massive and highly charged images of Auden's face—"that wedding cake left out in the rain"—had been commissioned for the exhibition, and Spender very much admired them. The poet had never seen a Swatch watch and was fascinated by the one the artist was wearing, especially because it had a rotating image of Mickey Mouse.

Another guest was Paul O'Grady, a brilliant Irish-American scholar whose work on Catholics in the reign of Henry VIII also interested Spender. Snatches of the conversation floated up the table, with O'Grady delivering this sentence supporting some point about Auden's Christianity: "I think Auden would agree that a melange of incoherent prejudices is very far removed from a firm Catholic theology, anti-papal or otherwise." One could see how such a man could get him around to talking about his relationship with Auden. An extraordinary revelation emerged: "Auden loved me, but he never really liked me." That provided much fuel for post-dinner speculation as the guests, including Caroline Delval, whose organisational and acute literary skills did much to make the exhibition successful, wandered off into the Vienna night. Later in a nearby bar Paul O'Grady and I gave full vent to our musings on what England's Poet Laureate could possibly have meant. We came to the same conclusion, that Auden indeed loved him, but what he didn't like about him was his abandoning his early flirtation with homosexuality and the fact that Auden had intended Spender to be the novelist of the "Auden generation," but he had disregarded that advice and went on with poetry.

By a happy coincidence, Auden's old friend Leonard Bernstein was in Vienna to conduct the Philharmonic, and when he heard about the exhibition, he asked for a guided tour. He ambled over from the Musikverein one afternoon with his assistant Aaron Stern. He spent an hour going through the exhibits in great detail and offered many piercing insights. When he came to a photograph of Auden and Chester

Auden and Chester Kallman in Venice, sitting outside Caffe Florian in Piazza San Marco, 1949. Photo by Stephen Spender.

Kallman, he stopped and said, "This photo tells you all you need to know about that relationship; there is Auden looking at Chester, and Chester is looking at the camera."

I sat him down to view a BBC documentary on Auden in which the closing sequence is footage of Auden's funeral. The Kirchstetten Village Brass Band is playing some sombre dirge, but the director chose to play as the soundtrack under the footage, a full orchestral version of "Siegfried's Funeral March."

The Author with Leonard Bernstein

Auden had requested that this be played at his funeral, and
Chester had played it on the gramophone in the Kirchstetten
house. Auden said he wanted "Siegfried's Funeral March and
not a dry eye in the house." He got his request. But now looking away from the television screen in the Künstlerhaus, Bernstein looked up and said: "Wow, not bad for a local village
band!" He recalled then that one of his own early orchestral
works, "The Age of Anxiety," was inspired by Auden's poem

Tangier, 1961: Standing, from left, William S. Burroughs, Allen Ginsberg, Alan Ansen,
Gregory Corso, and Ian Sommerville; sitting, Peter Orlovsky, left, and Paul Bowles.

of the same name. He recited memoriter, "September 1, 1939,"
while puffing with great dramatic effect on an untipped cigarette. He also recalled Auden's love of opera and the poet's
many librettos composed with Chester Kallman.

Soon after the Vienna exhibition, I travelled to Athens to
meet Alan Ansen, who first met Auden in New York when he
attended a series of lectures on Shakespeare given by Auden and
briefly became his unpaid amanuensis in 1948–49. Ansen was

educated at Harvard, where he took a first in classics. He had led a somewhat bohemian but scholarly life, enabled by an inheritance from an elderly aunt. He resolved never to take paid employment during his lifetime—a resolution he fulfilled with consummate skill and not a little judicious financial husbandry.

I knew that Auden held his intellect in high esteem and highly regarded his poetry. He acknowledges Ansen's help with "The Age of Anxiety" and *The Portable Greek Reader*. Ansen was a sort of muse figure to the Beat Generation and is the model for Rollo Greb in Jack Kerouac's *On the Road* and for AJ in William Burrough's *Naked Lunch*. Indeed he is credited with having typed the manuscript of *Naked Lunch* in Tangier.

He was in his sixties when I met him, and during the time I spent with him, I could still see traces of how Kerouac described Rollo Greb:

> He had more books than I've ever seen in all my life—two libraries, two rooms loaded from floor to ceiling around all four walls and such books as the Apocryphal Something-or-Other in ten volumes. He played Verdi operas and pantomimed them in his pyjamas with a great rip down the back. He didn't give a damn about anything. He is a great scholar who goes reeling down the New York waterfront with original seventeenth-century musical manuscripts under his arm, shouting. He crawls like a big spider through the streets. His excitement blew out of his eyes in stabs of fiendish light. He rolled his neck in spastic ecstasy. He could hardly get a word out he was so excited with life.

The library came with him from Long Island to Venice and Athens. He pointed out a chair that Chester Kallman gave him, which came from Auden's house in Kirchstetten.

Alan Ansen

"What should be done with this after I die" he asked me, more as a rhetorical question than one needing testamentary advice, for he was soon on to other subjects.

Over glasses of Cinzano Rosso, he told me of Chester's last days in Athens with a touching, genuine sadness in his face and voice. Tales of his drinking Ouzo from early morning, tales of his being robbed by Athenian rough trade, tales of insufferable loneliness drowned in a vat of drink. Ansen said he had "lost his criterion when Wystan died." He then recited some lines Chester had written about Auden's death:

> *Wystan is gone; a gift of fertile years*
> *And now of emptiness: I found him dead*
> *Turning icy blue on a hotel bed.*
>
> ...
>
> *I shared his work and life as best I could*
> *For both of us, often impatiently.*
> *So it was; let it be.*

He was pleased with the catalogue of the Vienna exhibition I brought for him and glad, he said, that Auden's adopted homeland remembered and honoured him.

What emerged from the Vienna exhibition and the international coverage it received was, above all, a sense that Auden's legend lived on in Austria. Yet, there was also this all-pervasive sense that Austria had claimed him as one of her own and a feeling that he would have been greatly pleased to be so claimed by the people he lived and died amongst. Some visitors to the exhibition mentioned that the Austrian tax office presented him with a tax demand so substantial that the shock of it shortened his life. Though the bill was eventually halved, it did cause Auden—a natural worrier about money—terrible distress. His letter to the tax office is a masterpiece explaining the poet's art, as are the lines from his poem "At the Grave of Henry James."

> *Master of nuance and scruple,*
> *Pray for me and for all writers living or dead;*
> *Because there are many whose works*
> *Are in better taste than their lives;*
> *Because there is no end*
> *To the vanity of our calling: make intercession*
> *For the treason of all clerks.*

Funeral Blues

*By mourning tongues
the death of the poet was kept from his poems.*

Saturday, September 29, 1973. A car travelling westward toward Vienna on the autobahn, which connects it to Linz, suddenly pulls into a lay-by. The driver and sole occupant is overcome by emotion. Austrian Radio has just announced the death of W.H. Auden in Vienna the previous evening.

The tall, elegant figure of Stella Musulin, for whom the phrase stiff upper lip might easily have been invented, suddenly looks frail and vulnerable. She grips the steering wheel tightly and only absorbs snippets of the broadcast. A line of Auden's echoes in her head: "The words of the dead man/ Are modified in the guts of the living." Stella contacted Auden just a few days earlier to offer him the use of her flat while he was in Vienna to give a poetry reading. Little did she realise, she now thought, that yesterday would be "his last afternoon as himself." Stella recalled the exchange of letters quite clearly. She remembered, too, how he had encouraged her to go to Linz because, as he put it, "she had heard it all before" and he admonished in a camp tone he reserved for close friends: "Mother says one must always stick to one's commitments."

Hotel Altenburgerhof Vienna where Auden died

Only the voice of Austrian historian Friederich Heer, drifting across the airwaves, talking about their mutual friend Auden in the past tense, jolts her back to the present. Other remembered lines from Auden's elegy on Yeats also helped to snap her out of her despair: "Now he is scattered among a hundred cities/ And wholly given over to unfamiliar affections/ To find his happiness in another kind of wood." She drives onward, leaving the autobahn and moving east toward Auden's house in the tiny hamlet of Kirchstetten.

She concentrates her thoughts on Chester Kallman, Auden's partner of thirty-three years. As Frederick Heer's doleful encomium filled the interior of her car, she began to focus on the wellbeing of the man for whom Auden once fleetingly entertained the notion of murdering someone out of jealous despair. "What are you howling about," Stella murmurs at the car radio, "what gives you the right to mourn for Wystan? Think of Chester." In Stella's view, it was impossible not to think of Chester; it was not so much a question of how much he would grieve over the death of Auden as how he would survive it.

Arriving at Auden's house, she hopes to find Chester Kallman. Instead, she finds the place shuttered and gloomy. Only the housekeeper's "wall-eyed mongrel" is there to greet her with wild, discordant barking. She stuck a hastily scribbled note on the shuttered door and looked around the garden. She left, closing the gate on which a small neatly engraved plaque contained the names: W.H. Auden over that of Chester Kallman. Turning to take a final look for any sign of life in Auden's house or the nearby housekeeper's cottage, she is met only by the dog's relentless "irritating falsetto."

The road westward out of Kirchstetten leads Stella on a journey of about thirty minutes before she reaches Ober-Grafendorf and her home in the grounds of Fridau Castle. There is little to distract her. She knows the road intimately. Only one landmark takes her mind off her concern about Chester's predicament. On a hill just off the road, she sees the ruin of a fourteenth-century Church dedicated to one of Auden's favourite holy women, Saint Cecilia. She recalls something of his poem, "Hymn for Saint Cecilia." She manages to muster some lines:

> *Blessed Cecilia, appear in visions*
> *To all musicians, appear and inspire:*
> *Translated Daughter, come down and startle*
> *Composing mortals with immortal fire.*

Ruin of the church dedicated to St Cecilia near Kirchstetten

Stella is far from calm as she paces the floor back at Fridau. Auden's last letter to her is on her desk. While exonerating her from being present at the Vienna poetry reading, it also expresses the wish to meet in a few days when he promises to "tell her all about it." Her reverie is disturbed by the ringing of the telephone. Auden's housekeeper, Frau Strobl, tells her that Chester Kallman wants her to come to tea tomorrow. She goes to bed secure in the knowledge that, at least for now, Chester is safe.

Sunday, September 30. Morning came with no tremendous pathetic fallacy heralding its arrival. No dark clouds gathered; no other ill omens attended the sad day. It was perfect autumn weather in Lower Austria. Stella goes about her morning routine and prepares to motor back to Auden's house. Recalling his oft-repeated mantra, "I wouldn't know how to be hungry if it were not for my watch," she set off aiming to arrive at Kirchstetten at the appointed hour for tea. According to the poet's reckoning, teatime, a rare enough social ritual in Auden's life, was precisely 4.15 pm. Now that he was dead, she was even more determined to honour the eccentricities of his devotion to routine. She remembered him saying, "Routine in an intelligent man is a sign of ambition." As she enters Auden's sitting room, the scene awaiting her has all the elements of a Central European version of bedlam colliding haphazardly with a French farce.

A thick fug of cigarette smoke enveloped the low-ceilinged room. These slightly impenetrable conditions were nothing new for Stella. She usually found Auden and Chester swathed in clouds of cigarette smoke. Chester's devotion to the culinary usefulness of the deep-fat fryer and Auden's refusal to even rarely open a window made for a perpetual caliginous miasma.

As Stella opened the door, multilingual babbling competed for airspace; Italian, English, and the sing-song of Austrian dialect mingled. Chester spotted Stella at the door and hurried over to hug her, saying, "The whole thing's terrible. You have to help me." It was a portent of what was to come

Auden, in his sitting room at Kirchstetten

in the days ahead when the house filled with deathwatch beetles. Stella knew from the slowness of his speech that Chester was doped by tranquillisers and alcohol. He and Auden believed in "the chemical life"; uppers in the morning and downers at bedtime.

Chester returned to where he was seated "in Auden's usual place," Stella notes. He made introductions where they were needed. She knew all present except Auden's and Chester's close friend, Thekla Clark, and her daughter, Lisa, who arrived from Florence that morning. Two callboys Chester brought back from Vienna seated on the floor smoking and drinking were, not surprisingly, also unknown to her. The mayor of Kirchstetten, the local head schoolmistress, Frau Maria Seitz, a Viennese filmmaker, Adolf Opel, Auden's housekeeper, Frau Strobl, and her son Franz made up the odd convocation. To Stella's intense annoyance, the Viennese escorts are not slow about offering their opinion on the arrangements for Auden's funeral. It is, after all, the sole topic for which this gathering has been convened.

The question divides not only the room but separates cultures, native and foreign, politics, local and national, and divergent Judeo-Christian values also get a look in. Anglicanism, high and low, even agnosticism, gets an inadvertent airing. To Stella, it seems as if the Council of Nicaea has reconvened in a cottage in Lower Austria. Each side competes, argues, and counterargues about how one of the twentieth century's greatest poets should be sent to his final resting place. Stella muses that Auden would have adored it. Before she ventures an opinion, Horace's famous line comes to her as an impish distraction: "As many men, as many opinions."

The mayor of Kirchstetten was a minor god within his own dominion. He was also a man not easily gainsaid. Josef Enzinger was tall, heavily built, sported a thick moustache, and was a bit of a dandy. He would not have been out of place in the wrestling ring. However, he had finally met his match in Auden's sitting room. The mayor argues the case for a full grand funeral with the utmost degree of pomp and circumstance the province of Lower Austria can muster. Pompes funébres was anathema to Chester but was relished by all other villagers in the room. After all, they were burying Kirchstetten's most distinguished citizen.

Mayor Enzinger encounters strong opposition from all sides of the room. The "widow" Auden is not for turning. Chester wants the funeral done and dusted as quickly as possible and with the minimum fuss. He already asked Auden's brother John and Stephen Spender to arrive on Tuesday. This hasty interment is totally unacceptable to the village luminaries who argue that they would not bury a dog as Kallman proposed, let alone one of the world's best-known poets. The views of a man who is essentially a Jewish agnostic outsider will not, it seems, be allowed to prevail over those of the very conservative Catholic elders of Kirchstetten.

In utter despair and now rather sozzled and doped, Chester exits the room and leaves the bickering party to their heated exchanges. Stella recalled that the mayor looked annoyed, Frau Seitz worried, and Mrs. Clark bewildered. A conclusion had to be reached soon because Auden's family, friends, and the world's media were awaiting news of the funeral arrangements. The unseemly fight over the poet's body was no less intense than that between Satan and the Archangel Michael over the body of Moses.

Mayor Enzinger had one final ace up his sleeve. Austria was still run by a labyrinthine tangle of ancient rules and regulations, many unchanged since the days of empire. The death of a foreign national on Austrian soil came with complications, even in normal circumstances. The death of a fa-

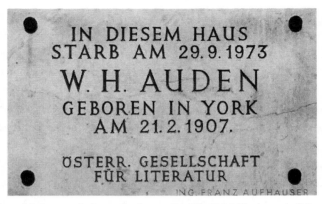

Memorial plaque to Auden on the former site of the Hotel Altenburgerhof Vienna

mous foreign national in a Viennese hotel room where a half-empty bottle of vodka and a quantity of sleeping pills lay on the bedside table intimated a possible suicide in the eyes of local officialdom. This represented nothing out of the ordinary to anyone who knew Auden well. His belief in the chemical life was second only to his belief in the efficacy of alcohol. For most of his later life, a glass of vodka sat on his night table by his bedside. Should he wake in the night, he would take a gulp and settle back to sleep in preparation for his invariably early rising time.

Here, amidst the quagmire of Austrian red tape, Herr Enzinger struck his most lethal blow. He informed everyone present, somewhat disingenuously, that his political influence alone could secure the release of the body for burial six days hence. The burly figure of the mayor rose from his place to indicate the meeting was over. Thus it was announced that W.H. Auden would be laid to rest in a "grave of honour" in the Catholic cemetery of Kirchstetten on Thursday, October 4.

Monday, September 30 – Wednesday, October 3. Stella Musulin now prepares to do battle with the monolithic bulwark of Austrian officialdom. She is well-equipped for the task.

Something about her presence fitted the Irish portmanteau description "a woman of capernosity and function." She was, after all, the daughter-in-law of the man who helped write the ultimatum to Serbia on behalf of Emperor Franz Joseph. Though she cared little for this part of her family history, it still carried great sway in Viennese official circles.

While Auden's brother, Dr. John Auden, and Thekla Clarke were busy pleading with the American Embassy to help release Auden's body, Stella quietly and discreetly made a few phone calls to high places. Thus she managed to secure the release of the poet's remains for burial on Thursday, October 4. If only the internecine conflict had ended there, all would have fared well for Auden on his onward journey. The debate about the funeral arrangements dragged on over the next few days, and divergent views were still scattered around, as Stella amusingly put it "like snuff at a wake."

Chester disappeared into an alcohol-induced haze, thus silently consenting to any arrangements the interested parties devised. Amid all the confrontation and gloom, Stella managed to cheer Chester up by telling him only a few years ago, the village, according to the local custom, would have arranged for a local girl to dress up in white for the funeral procession as a token "bride" for the bachelor Auden. No villager knew of his marriage of convenience to Thomas Mann's daughter, Erika, in 1935, thus making him a widower, as they were technically still married when she predeceased him in 1969. Stella felt that Auden was having a serious belly laugh from his place in the Elysian Fields or wherever he was.

Friends of Auden, many from the world of English letters, began arriving in Kirchstetten ahead of the funeral. Stephen Spender, Sonia Orwell, Charles Montieth of Faber & Faber, Alan Ansen from Greece, Edward Mendelson, Auden's literary executor, and David Luke, representing Auden's Oxford

College, Christ Church. Peter Müller of the International Auden Society entertained many of the arrivals. The village had never seen anything quite like it. The village inn, much frequented by Auden, did a roaring trade. Its limited menu prompted one visiting dignitary to vow never again to eat gulyás, that great staple of Central European cuisine.

Thursday, October 4. Thursday's slightly chilly autumnal weather required some mourners to wear topcoats. The heartier among them, including Chester, braved the day in coat jackets. Stella noted that "Chester wore his grief with a certain dignity." As is usual at such country funerals, some mourners stood outside the house, too shy or perhaps respectful to go inside. Auden's open coffin was in his bedroom, the head end raised for mourners to bid a final farewell to the deceased. Some touched his crossed hands; others lightly kissed his brow.

Now it was Stella's turn to say goodbye to her friend. As she entered the room, she recalled later how Auden's spiritual presence struck her with great force. "It was Wystan Auden, out-distancing now all his human frailty, remote and unknowable as perhaps he always was." Chester was the last out of the room as the undertakers sealed the coffin. Moving to the sitting room where a select group of mourners had gathered, he fulfilled one of Auden's wishes for his funeral. He asked for "Siegfried's Funeral March and not a dry eye in the house." Both requests were fulfilled. While the wife of a former Viennese rentboy named Hugi, whom Auden befriended, sobbed intermittently as Wagner's lament blared from a scratchy record on the phonograph, others looked on in curious disbelief.

Stella observed the lengthy cortège which now led from the house and saw its constitution as adequately representative of the life led by Auden and Kallman. She impishly mus-

Auden's funeral procession at Kirchstetten

es as she sees the tall white-haired figure of Stephen Spender that he may have had Auden in mind when he wrote those memorable lines: "I think continually of those who were truly great... Born of the sun, they travelled a short while toward the sun/And left the vivid air signed with their honour."

The hearse leaves the house preceded by the Kirchstetten Brass Band making a valiant attempt at playing "The Dead March" from *Saul*. The distance from the house to the church is about half a mile. At a road junction in the village, the coffin is transferred from a hearse to a bier carried by the undertakers. Here the Church takes over from the State. Auden's remains are passed to the Anglican chaplain from the British Embassy in Vienna and to the local Catholic curate. Holy Water is sprinkled on the coffin, bearing a single large wreath with a black ribbon which reads "From Chester." The Catholic curate is garbed in black funeral vestments, and on his head, the tasselled silk biretta abandoned since the Second Vatican Council in most parishes in the Catholic world. The Anglican chaplain raises an arm in simple blessing.

The procession moves slowly toward the eighteenth century onion-domed church, past fruit trees still groaning under the weight of autumnal abundance, past cottage gates where resident dogs meet the distinguished gathering with excited yelping. A thurifer, wielding a golden censer, fills the air with incense as he swings to and fro, with practised precision, the burning embers of charcoal. Ahead of him, a young acolyte carries a plain processional cross.

The parishioners of Kirchstetten are about to witness perhaps the strangest event in the parish's long ecclesiastical history. The church service for Auden is to be ecumenical. Many in attendance considered it a mortal sin for a Catholic to enter a Protestant church. The presence of a Protestant clergyman on the altar of their own place of worship caused many tongues to wag disapprovingly in this small farming community. Some, fearing for their mortal souls, stood outside the entrance.

The interior of the Church is in a simple, unpretentious Gothic style. It is dedicated to Saint Vitus, the patron saint of dancers and protector against lightning and oversleeping. Auden attended Sunday mass here, tunelessly bellowing out the hymns from the organ loft. Today, even that loft is crowded to the rafters for his funeral.

The curate and the vicar deliver the readings in English and German. To English ears, there is nothing unusual in the bilingual inter-denominational service. The Rev. Bruce Duncan reads from the Book of Common Prayer, the extended version of the Letter of Saint Paul to the Corinthians, chapter 15, verses 20-58: "O death, where is thy sting? O grave, where is thy victory?"

No graveside oration is delivered. Auden is spared the child bride, and no hunter blows a horn wishing him happy hunting in the Elysian Fields. The only reference to his

Auden's coffin. Chester Kallman on the extreme right.
Photo by Stella Musulin.

calling is a few lines from Rilke read by an official of the Lower Austrian government. The burial occurs in a grave of honour inside the Churchyard gate. Today a simple iron cross marks the place. A small plaque reads in raised iron-work W.H. Auden 1907–1973 Poet and Man of Letters. The mourners disperse.

That night Auden appears to Stella in a dream in which the two friends debate aspects of Martin Luther's transla-tions of sacred texts. Auden is quoting, "...and the dead shall be raised incorruptible." In mid-sentence, he vanishes. Stel-la is now wide awake.

Stella was invariably an early riser. It was an old habit; boarding school, hush-hush work during the war, proximi-ty to a demanding Churchill at that time, and a long-stand-ing antipathy towards sloth. This morning was different. Startled by Auden's appearance and sudden disappearance in her dream, she feared that her memory of him might fade. She stayed in bed later than usual. She lay there recollecting

Auden's grave in the churchyard at Kirchstetten

fragments of what he had told her about his first arrival in Kirchstetten. Before she had taken breakfast, she searched out the occasional notes she was in the habit of writing down after some of her meetings with Auden. To do so frequently she considered an intrusive impertinence. Quite soon, she had a clear idea of what he told her during that first meeting shortly after he arrived in Lower Austria. She was confident from the hasty perusal that it was all about the quest for home.

Leaving the Mezzogiorno
Finding Home

*...what I dared not hope or fight for
is, in my fifties, mine, a toft-and-croft
where I needn't, ever, be at home to*

*those I am not at home with, not a cradle,
a magic Eden without clocks,
and not a windowless grave, but a place
I may go both in and out of.*

James Joyce, patron saint of perpetual literary exile, was fond of saying that he had to leave home so that he might find home. Like Joyce, Auden was in search of home for most of his life. Similar to Joyce's father, who moved his family around Dublin (though for entirely different reasons), Auden's father moved his family of three boys around the north of England, ultimately with some damaging consequences, especially for Wystan, the middle son of the three. From his birth in a house in York on February 21, 1907 until he bought, aged fifty, his first property in Austria in 1957, Auden was searching for home. For him, however, home would never be just a house; instead, it was a perception, a feeling of finally reaching a particular destination that altered the way he felt about the world and about himself.

He began his search in earnest in 1957 after winning Italy's most prestigious literary prize. The Feltrinelli Award for literature secured him about 350,000 US dollars in today's values. It was the most significant sum of money he had at any time in his life. For the previous ten years, Auden rented a house on the Island of Ischia in the fishing village of Forio. In the 1940s, Ischia was untouched by mass tour-ism. It was not, however, untouched by war. The island was bombed twice during World War II. The first was on September 8, 1943, by the British; the second time, on the 17th of that month, at the hands of the German Luftwaffe. They struck the historic centre of Forio and the port of Ischia and there followed the inevitable death and destruction.

In the post-war period, Forio became something of an artistic haven. It was unusual for the Nordic Auden to go south when thus far, going north in search of his roots had been part of his very identity since early youth. Even in exile in America in 1947, he would write: "... years before I ever went there, the North of England was the Never-Never Land of my dreams. Nor did those feelings disappear when I finally did: to this day, Crewe Junction marks the wildly exciting frontier where the alien South ends and the North, my world, begins."

Ischia also had a long tradition of literary visitors. Stendhal was there in 1817 and lodged happily in a peasant's house. Alphonse de Lamartine, best remembered for his novel *Graziella*, was there three years later. During his stay on Ischia, he was visited by his friend Eugène Pelletan, the French politician and journalist. He convinced De Lamartine to publish the tragic love story inspired by Italy. Henrik Ibsen worked on his play *Peer Gynt* on the island in 1867.

Early on in their friendship, Auden described to Stella what he found so attractive about Ischia when he began spending his summers on the island from April 1949. He told her he responded to its "geological structure" in a way one would expect from the author of *In Praise of Limestone*. At the island's core rests an extinct volcano, Mount Epomeo, whose ever-threatening presence Auden found exhilarating. He imagined that at any moment, the island might "betray her secret fever" and not behave as was expected of her restorative

Old postcard of Forio

waters to "make limber the gout-stiffened joint/And improve the venereal act."

The green isle, *L'isola Verde*, is what the Ischians call it. Auden occasionally referred to it by its Latin name, Aenaria, meaning land of wine. He enjoyed telling his house guests that viniculture had been essential to the island's identity since wine was first produced there in 700 BC. The island's place in ancient legend was secured long ago. The banishment from Olympus imposed by Jupiter on the troublesome colossus Tifeo, such legends tell us, occasioned his abandoned body to be used for the island's formation.

When Auden arrived, Homeric legends were still told on Ischia with enthusiasm normally reserved for recounting gossip told about an incident in a local bar the previous evening. *The Shield of Achilles,* published during his time on Ischia, was almost certainly inspired by his time on the island. The dark dystopian imagery on the shield of Auden's imagination is in stark contrast to what Auden found in this bucol-

Auden in a US Army major's uniform, with Tania Stern

ic Eden, which was, in reality, more redolent of what Achilles's mother, Thetis, wished to see engraved on the shield commissioned for her son. The horror Auden had seen in his role as a major with the post-war US Strategic Bombing Survey still inclined him towards a not entirely rose-tinted view of the world.

Stella remembered him telling her how tired he had become of big-city life. This is reflected in his poem "Ischia" which he wrote soon after arriving on the island:

> *Dearest to each his birthplace; but to recall a green*
> *valley where mushrooms fatten in the summer nights*
> *and silvered willows copy*
> *the circumflexions of the stream*

> *is not my gladness today: I am presently moved*
> *by sun-drenched Parthenopea, my thanks are for you,*
> *Ischia, to whom a fair wind has*
> *brought me rejoicing with dear friends*
> *from soiled productive cities.*

Stella was quite adept at understanding esoteric references and was not shy about asking when she did not understand something. She recalled asking him why, in his Ischia poem, sun-drenched parasitic barnacles could possibly enchant him. It may have been the defining moment in what was to become a very close friendship. It might even have been, Stella recalled, "the moment when he decided to treat me as, perhaps, if not an intellectual equal, then at least not a total idiot!"

Fate, rather than design, brought Auden and Kallman to Ischia in 1948. Once they had finished the libretto commissioned for Stravinsky's *The Rake's Progress*, they decided to set sail from New York for Europe. Auden wanted Chester to see England. Chester had a greater desire to see Prague. During the trip, they visited Auden's father, who was then living in the Lake District. Dr. Auden was not altogether taken by the precocious Kallman. Chester soon became tired of what he perceived as staid English manners and snobbishness, and Auden took him off to Austria. Auden had stayed in the ski resort of Kitzbühel as a boy, and, he later claimed, it was here that he lost his virginity. It was to a comely innkeeper called Hedwig Petzold to whom the honour of deflowering the sixteen-year-old Auden fell. She would, years later, be an important factor, though of the more practical kind, in his decision to move to live in Austria.

While staying in Naples, Auden and Kallman decided to take a ferry to the island, the largest in the Bay of Naples. It

Hedwig Petzold and her husband

is a journey of a mere 18 nautical miles or one hour's sailing
time. They immediately liked what they saw. One of their
first stops was the tiny town of Forio, on the island's western
side. Here they took rooms at the Pensione Nettuno. They ex-
plored the island from the village and found it so agreeable,
especially its lack of English tourists, that Auden decided to
rent a house at 22 Via Santa Lucia. They soon established the
old pattern of Auden writing and Kallman housekeeping or
rather, cooking. Auden and Kallman were completely obliv-
ious to their domestic surroundings and shared a common
gene which gave them an aesthetic bypass at birth. All who
knew them noticed this and cared as little as they did about
interior decorative frippery. To be in Auden's presence was
more than sufficient compensation for what Stella called the
"squalor" in which they usually lived. Auden rarely possessed

more than one suit, and when he wore it friends recalled him "looking like an unmade bed."

For the first time since living at home with his parents in England, Auden had the services of domestic help in Forio. The exchange rate of the US dollar against the Italian lira in post-war Italy afforded them the opportunity to live a most comfortable life in Italy. Dining in local restaurants and drinking vast quantities of Ischian wine was possible at a cost which made New York seem hideously expensive. Auden immediately set up headquarters at a local cafe called Bar Mari or, sometimes more grandly, Caffé International. It was situated on Forio's central square. Here he observed, with the poet's eye, the flotsam and jetsam of local life as it passed by and held court to all comers, some drawn by his intellect, others by his wads of US dollars.

There was no shortage of intellectual company in Forio in the early 1950s. The American painter, Carlyle Brown, befriended Auden at this time. Brown was greatly influenced by the Russian painter Pavel Tchelitchew, who encouraged him to travel in Italy. Auden liked this down-to-earth former US naval officer who introduced him to other painters living on the island, including Leonardo Cremonini. Francis Bacon was a great admirer of Cremonini and encouraged Erica Brausen, the founder of the prestigious Hanover Gallery in London, to get Auden to write an article about him.

Eduard Bargheer, a talented German painter, banned by the Nazis as a "degenerate" artist, also met Auden in Forio. Carlo Levi, author of *Christ Stopped at Eboli*, writes of Bargheer's eloquent description of Ischia at this time:

Above all, I liked the way he spoke of Ischia, of Epomeo, of quarries and caves, of fishermen and shepherds, and of the rural gods, who share bread with them and

Maria Sense, owner of Bar Maria in Forio, with Auden

rest outdoors shadow of figs; of that world of the poor, of loneliness and enchantment, where the bizarre goat is queen, and the sea and the earth are full of invisible presences, continuously mixed with the smallest daily events. We were in the middle of the war, and this young German thought and spoke as if ferocity, division, and absurd madness did not exist and did not touch him: nor did he complain of how much he himself had suffered from it.

Others would soon discover Auden's Ischian Eden. Visconti, Truman Capote, and Sir William Walton were some of the luminaries who made their way to the island. But for now, from the late forties to the late fifties, it was largely Auden's preserve, and with few exceptions, he did not engage in any meaningful way with foreigners. One such exclusion from his rule was a brilliant young American poet, Anthony Hecht. He first met Hecht in New York in 1951. He served with the 97th Infantry Division and saw active service in Europe. Hecht's most horrifying experience was his involvement with the liberation of the Flossenburg concentration camp in Bavaria in April 1945. He introduced Auden to his friend Thekla Clark, who frequently holidayed on Ischia when Auden lived there. Thekla Clark and her daughter Lisa were to become an important part of Auden's life in the years ahead. He even contemplated proposing marriage to Clark at one point. Her reaction was: "What would a distinguished middle-aged homosexual writer want with a giddy young woman?"

Eduard Bargheer, *Fishing boats in Forio* (1947)

Thekla Clark was brilliant at observing the roles played by foreigners on Ischia, especially those chosen for them by the locals. She also observed how those put to the test lived up to how they were perceived.

"We played the parts assigned to us, our unpronounceable names changed by the Forians into indicators like *lo scrittore*, the writer; *lo studioso*, the scholar; I was *la biondona*, the big blonde. The important thing was to play the parts well. It was as though we lived in the third person; we were what we appeared to be to others. Wystan studied it, I revelled in it, and Chester accepted it unquestioningly."

It was on Ischia that Auden's famously lined face began to appear to the world. Fair-haired and fair-skinned when he arrived in 1948, ten years later, that self-described "wedding cake left out in the rain" was already a work in progress. The condition was aided by the consumption of substantial quantities of vodka and wine and smoking two packets of cigarettes a day. Add the smorgasbord of pharmaceutical uppers and downers to the equation, and you have the recipe

Prince Heinrich of Hesse-Kassel aka Enrico D'Assia. One of Auden's painter friends on Ischia

Auden's friend Anthony Hecht

for one of the most famous faces in the world. A friend once remarked: "One of these days, we'll have to pull the wrinkles back to see if he's still in there."

For most of a decade, Forio proved to be exactly what Auden was seeking by way of a retreat from New York; a place where he could, with intermittent domestic disruptions, concentrate on his writing. He employed an entirely unsuitable houseboy called Giocondo Sacchetti, who shared much of Chester's dislike of domesticity and, in equal measure, his petulance. He was named "Gigolocondo" by some of Auden's guests. His youth and brooding Italian good looks, coupled with his willingness and availability, made him an appealing quantity for visiting homosexuals. His indolence led to tension in the Auden household. He would eventually be one

Ruin of the Cathedral of Our Lady of the Assumption, Ischia

of the reasons for Auden's departure from the island under a sordid miasma of claim and counterclaim as the citizenry of Forio took sides in what became known as the "Giocondo scandal."

In the earlier halcyon days on Ischia, Auden began to explore the island in great detail. Known to friends as a highly reckless driver, against all advice, he bought a Vespa scooter. A collision on one of his adventures very nearly cost him an eye. Ischia's churches and religious rituals held a particular fascination for him. The ruin of the Cathedral of Our Lady of the Assumption overlooking the Bay of Sant'Anna was one of Auden's favourite vantage points on the island.

A more macabre place of funereal interest he found beneath the Church of the Immaculate Conception.

Here, dead nuns were laid, or rather seated, to rest in a collection of low vaulted rooms called a putridarium. It contains high-backed stone throne-like chairs on which the dead sisters' bodies were seated. As the flesh slowly decomposed, the putrefying liquids were collected by novices in stone jars beneath the seat, and finally, the dried skeletons were placed in an ossuary. This ancient practice was grounded in the belief in the uselessness of the body as anything other than an earthly receptacle for the soul. Auden relished telling this ghoulish tale after dinner.

An enchanted island does not stay enchanted forever. Thekla Clark put a searching question to Auden many years after the idyl had ended. She asked if he had really been that

Putridarium, Castello Aragonese, Ischia

Tom Driberg and Guy Burgess (right) in Moscow

enchanted foreigner on Ischia trying to belong. He replied: "Yes, and that is why I had to leave."

There were more pressing reasons which hastened his departure soon after his fiftieth birthday in February 1957. The birthday was a happy event enlivened by the presence of old friends and a congratulatory telegram from Guy Burgess in Moscow. Burgess was a friend from the 1930s, and both men had considerable respect for each other's intellects if, not always, political views. Auden had toyed with Communism in the 1930s and is sometimes still misrepresented as a Communist poet. By 1940 he had made the heady journey from Christ to Marx and back to Christ again. By then, his poetry was beginning to be more concerned with the redemptive power of love than with any political ideology.

Had that birthday telegram arrived in 1951, it may have given MI5 and MI6 even more reason to suspect Auden of having some involvement in Burgess's escape plan. A seriously bungled attempt to embroil Auden in Burgess's flight to Moscow reads like a terrible farce. That, coupled with some bad news reporting when the British state papers on the Burgess affair were released days after the centenary of Auden's birth, all contrived to present Auden as "a wanted man" at the time. Before the unmasking of Burgess as a Soviet agent, Auden had invited his old friend to Ischia, an invitation which subsequent events obviously prevented from being fulfilled. People who visited Burgess in Moscow reported him often asking: "How is Auden? Have you seen him?"

Why, then would Auden ever want to leave this paradise? In 1956 his houseboy Giocondo attempted to cash a salary cheque for 600,000 lire. Whether the extra zero was forged or mistakenly added by Auden, the bank refused to cash it because there wasn't a credit balance sufficient to do so. Giocondo insisted the extra money was for services rendered and went around telling anyone who would listen that Auden, fearful of his partner Chester Kallman's jealousy, had reneged on his gift. This poisoned the air, coupled with the fact that his landlord, "a certain Monte," upon hearing that Auden had just won the Feltrinelli Prize, had jacked up the asking price of the place well beyond what it was worth. Auden had wished to buy the house. His father's death on May 3, 1957, the row with Giocondo, and an influx of English homosexuals combined to precipitate his exit. There was one other factor. He received a letter from Hedwig Petzold in Kitzbühel, which contained a newspaper cutting about a farmhouse for sale in Lower Austria.

This part of Austria had been in the Russian zone of occupation, and after the departure of the Russians, property prices were at an all-time low. For Auden, with his Feltrinelli bounty in the bank, it was a perfect opportunity to finally put down roots and for a reasonable sum of money. The vendor, a Mr. Erich Zimmerman, asked the Austrian Schilling equivalent of about 8,500 dollars for the house and roughly an acre of land. The house was purchased jointly in the names of Wystan Hugh Auden and Chester Simon Kallman, both residents of New York. The deal was concluded on December 9, 1957.

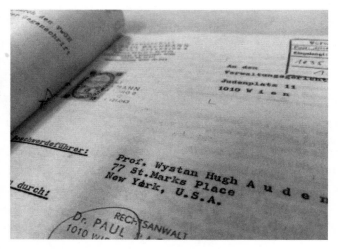

Legal documentation regarding the sale of the Kirchstetten House

W. H. Auden Buys Austrian House

W. H. Auden has bought himself a peasant's house in a remote village of lower Austria reports the Vienna newspaper, "Neues Oesterreich."

Auden said he paid for the house (near the village of Kirchstetten about 25 miles east of Vienna), with the proceeds of the Italian lyric prize recently awarded him.

"I have found real peace here and my work has gone ahead better than I ever thought possible," he stated in an interview.

Auden was mentally and emotionally prepared to move to the first and only house he would ever own. His decision to move "north" to the imagined hinterland of his youth was predicated by a desire to be in a German-speaking, wine-producing, opera-loving country. Austria fitted all three criteria perfectly. In Austria, he would make the last of many close female friendships. This one with Stella Musulin was intellectually the most significant of all.

Stella

Küss die Hand Frau Baronin—"I kiss your hand Baroness"

"She was very close to Auden," Peter Müller told me as we arrived in the courtyard of a building which predated the baroque Schloss Fridau at Ober-Grafendorf, some twenty-five kilometres from Auden's house at Kirchstetten. The castle, a ghostly presence in the distance, was occupied by the

The courtyard at Fridau Castle
where Stella had her flat

Interior of Fridau Castle before the occupation by Soviet troops

Russians at the end of World War II and left in a completely uninhabitable state. The soldiers used the eighteenth-century bindings in the library to mend their boots. Most of the furniture was looted or burned. The family moved to the adjacent semi-derelict wing of an earlier building where servants once lived and horses were stabled, to rooms made elegant by unpretentious good taste.

Later, when I was introduced to family and friends at Fridau, I realised it was akin to meeting entries from the Almanach de Gotha in the flesh. The ancestors of these people had been significant figures in the glory days of the Austro-Hungarian Empire. But for now, I was meeting a woman who, in Peter Müller's conspiratorial whisper, had been "very close to Auden."

The quadrangular configuration of this Austrian rural Eden had the feel of a small Oxbridge college. In the wing we now entered, a staircase led to a long corridor, at the end of which lay Stella Musulin's rooms. The door to these rooms was open in welcome, and this delicate, almost fragile woman stood with a ready, courteous, and friendly welcome. While Müller engaged in the courtly ritual of *küss die Hand Frau Baronin*—"I kiss your hand Baroness"—I was aware of her looking at me as if to take an initial reading of the cut of my jib. I learned later that such a reading was at once a natural instinctive reflex, for she had been an active operative for British Intelligence during World War II. I once asked her if she thought someone among our mutual acquaintances was a spy, and she replied, with a twinkle in her eye: "I am quite sure he is; there is something about the back of his neck."

She spoke perfectly accentless German to Müller, and when she switched to English, her voice was that kind of English upper-class RP that used to define a whole class. De-

The old wing where Stella lived at Fridau Castle

brett records her as directly descended from a ninth-century Welsh king. Though her upbringing was in that part of Wales known as "Little England," she proudly claimed her Celtic ancestry. She never engaged in any form of tiresome nationalistic jingoism. I knew her to be the author of two important books on Austrian history: *Vienna in the Age of Metternich* and *Austria: People and Landscape*. Auden wrote the Introduction to the latter.

Stella met Auden soon after he bought the Kirchstetten house in 1957. They were introduced by Hugo von Hofmanstal's daughter, Christiane Zimmer, a university lecturer in Vienna. Correspondence between them from the period shows that Auden and Stella had settled almost immediately into an easy friendship. Notes passed to and fro setting dates for lunches at Kirchstetten or at Fridau. So comfortable had the friendship become that before one luncheon at Fridau, Auden insisted that she come down to the courtyard to look at his VW car. He then showed her a hole in the car's bodywork, which he proudly announced as "a bullet hole." Auden habitually gave his car on loan when he was away from Kirchstetten. On the last occasion he did so, it was stolen and used in a robbery. He was immensely proud of the latest addition to the many dents resulting from less dramatic uses of his car. His driving skills were the subject of good-natured humour in and around the Kirchstetten hinterland. Someone once explained his tendency to ignore a red traffic signal by saying that he possessed such supreme self-confidence that when he came to a traffic light, he expected it to be green.

Auden came to rely on Stella's impeccable German for translations of things such as speeches he had to deliver on official occasions in Austria. He was also in the habit of sending her drafts of his poems in his letters to her. This is something he reserved for close friends whose opinions he valued.

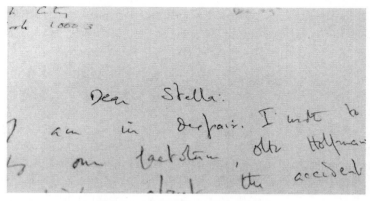

Auden's handwriting from a letter to Stella

It began when he was an undergraduate, often sending his drafts to Christopher Isherwood and Stephen Spender. He continued the practice throughout his writing life.

To illustrate Auden's personality, Stella told the story of a lunch party at Fridau where her young son Marko was also present. Advising the boy that a famous poet was coming to lunch and no doubt also advising best behaviour, she was surprised that her son's curiosity led him to ask Auden what exactly a poet does. She then recalled how this colossus of English poetry sat and explained in terms that a young boy could understand exactly what a poet does. Stella felt this was a mark of Auden's great humanity and kindness.

Auden also came to rely on Stella in the more intimate area of his personal relationship with Chester Kallman. Keeping Chester in purdah was an impossible task. He was, Stella recalled, "addicted to promiscuity." When Kallman sometimes disappeared into the miasma of homosexual bars in Vienna for long periods, Auden occasionally telephoned Stella to seek help in finding him. She had a pied-a-terre in the city. She recalled searching the seedy bars of the Linke Wien Zeile late at night for the straying Kallman. Apparently, her gentle admonishment, "Now Chester, time to go home," always worked, and she would then return the prodigal to Kirchstetten and Auden the next day. She felt that it could not have been easy for Chester to live in the shadow of this genius whose life was lived to a rigid, sacrosanct, and almost inviolable timetable.

She felt sympathy for Kallman's role, which was seen by less sympathetic observers as second fiddle to the great man. Especially by those completely lacking sympathy and understanding of the true nature of the relationship, he was seen as a sponger. She also remarked on the importance of Auden's role in Kallman's life when she recalled that after Auden's death, Chester had "lost his signpost in life" and began to disintegrate rapidly. A home movie made by a neighbour shortly after Auden's death shows Chester in a company at the dining table in Kirchstetten. He looked like a complete shadow of his former robust image. Here now was a broken man, adrift and lost like the lighthouse of Portus. Stella was always willing to give him credit for the role he played in Auden's life and ready to point out that he made sacrifices, not least amongst them a certain loss of dignity which came from being financed by Auden for most of his life. Stella's description of Chester as "a Dorian Grey figure, sparkling and damned, hero and victim, immature and over-ripe, sensitive and heartless, a man capable of loving and being loved" is the best we have of that complex figure.

* * *

The journey from Ober-Grafendorf to Schloss Fridau is, in Richard Bassett's colourful expression "a mere biscuit's throw." Bassett was *The Times* correspondent based in Vienna, covering an extensive part of East Central Europe for the paper. I arranged a meeting with Stella at Fridau. She was always interested in meeting journalists covering a region she knew and wrote so much about as a journalist herself. Bassett arrived two hours late because the "mere biscuit's throw" became an extended marathon. He missed the stop at Ober-Grafendorf and alighted miles further on. Undaunted, he trekked over a local hill across newly-mown fields and eventually arrived at Fridau. It was a sweltering summer's day, and Stella complimented him on surviving the journey, clad as he was in a heavy tweed jacket, stout pair of corduroy trousers, and, most remarkably, his necktie still in place.

Stella was curious to meet Richard. He had a reputation in Vienna as a man of strong opinions who was never reticent in expressing them. His description of Austrian women as "being rather like the buildings; either overrestored or sadly neglected" caused not a few elderly dowagers in Vienna to call for the smelling salts. Stella was intrigued by this and also by his description of Ceaușescu as a man who "even by the lax standards of modern psychiatry is surely certifiable."

Bassett had read Stella's much-praised book on Metternich. The conversation soon turned to Austria in those thirty-three

Richard Bassett with Zita the last Empress of Austria in 1982 at Waldstein Castle, Styria, the home of her daughter and son-in-law © Stefan Amsuess

years after the Napoleonic Wars, often defined as the Age of Metternich. The rise of Hungarian nationalism was also a key part of the discussion. Stella held a view on Vienna best represented by an article she wrote for *History Today* in 1978:

> A less revolutionary people than the Viennese could hardly be imagined. Broadly speaking, they consisted of court and society and the satisfiers of their needs, of civil servants trained in unquestioning loyalty and obedience, and intellectuals—scholars and writers whose social function was at that time in no way understood by authority. Then there were the students, an unorganized and totally unrevolutionary working class, and, finally, a highly explosive but equally unorganized and leaderless proletariat.

Stella defended Metternich's two-sided approach of, on the one hand, defending the Habsburg monarchy as its pow-

Stella's parents-in-law on their engagement

er ebbed and, on the other, trying to offer something to as-
suage the nationalist's demands. I made a strong case for the
Hungarian nationalists and the eventual key role played by
Count Gyula Andrássy and Ferenc Deák in brilliantly nego-
tiating the compromise of 1867, which saved the Habsburgs
to live to fight another day.

We also spoke of that "other day," June 28, 1914, in Sarajevo. Stella's father-in-law, Baron Alexander von Musulin
de Gomirje, was one of the principal architects of the ultimatum to Serbia following the assassination of Franz Ferdinand. Stella mentioned that he must have felt residual guilt
because he had a part Serbian background. His grandfather,
Alexander, founded the Slavic-Illyrian Reading Society in
Croatia as the Hungarian Revolution was about to get underway in 1848. Stella's father-in-law was loyal to the Habsburgs. He had every reason to be. He received preferment
in the Dual Monarchy based on his considerable diplomat-
ic achievements. He was appointed to Dresden, Paris, Stutt-
gart, Paris, Bucharest, Athens, and St. Petersburg as a rising
diplomat in the foreign service of the empire. After the out-
break of the Great War, he was made head of the new Department of War. With the war's end came the end of his ca-
reer. In 1919, with the abolition of titles, his name became
Musulin. Stella used that form of the name for her journal-
ism and books.

The family took its baronial title von Musulin de Gomirje from the Croatian settlement of Gomirje in north-western
Croatia. They had lands nearby, and Alexander's father, Lieutenant General Fieldmarshal Emil von Musulin, was born
in the region, further strengthening the family's links to
the Habsburg Kingdom. It was under Habsburg suzerainty
since 1527 when the Croatian nobility decided to accept Ferdinand I as their king.

Stella's books are still widely read by British historians interested in Habsburg and Austrian history. Philip Mansel, historian and a co-founder of The Society for Court Studies, visited Stella at Fridau. They struck up an immediate rapport. Stella claimed kinship with him "on the Welsh side." She was related to a family called Colvile-Mansel, and they had Welsh roots. This amused them both. Stella's pedigree in

Friedrich Heer, Chester Kallman, and Auden in Kirchstetten

those sometimes unreliable, weighty tomes, the stud books registering pedigree of the landed gentry, records her earliest ancestor as Rhodri, King of Wales, in the ninth century. She took this with a pinch of salt, believing firmly in Oscar Wilde's famous dictum: "You should study the Peerage ... it's the best thing in fiction the English have ever done." Stella was interested in the Ottoman's one-hundred-and-fifty-year rule over the Hungarians and, of course, the unsuccessful Siege of Vienna. On these subjects, Mansel's scholarly knowledge delighted her. They both liked the works of

Stella and her husband Janko soon after their marriage

Friedrich Heer, who was one of the most formidable Austrian intellectuals of the twentieth century. Heer befriended Auden, and they saw quite a good deal of each other in Vienna and Kirchstetten.

Mansel touched on the personal with Stella. That was rather unusual because she always resisted any encroachment on her personal life. Speaking of her relationship with her husband, from whom she was separated, she told him "we knew each other's parameters." Then she dropped the subject as quickly as it had been raised.

In June 1946, Stella married Baron Johann Emil Alexander von Musulin de Gomirje, better known in by-then-titleless Austria as Janko Musulin. There was little more than a year between them in age; she was born in 1915, and he in 1916. He was a significant figure in resisting the Nazi occupation of Austria, as was his friend Friedrich Heer, with whom he had been to school. Both were active in the Austrian resistance from the time of the Anschluss in March 1938. It consisted of disparate groups who fought to counter the general population's apathy towards the annexation of their homeland. It was organised under various charismatic characters

Stella's wedding. Front row from the left: Lavender Goddard Wilson, Stella's father-in-law Alexander von Musulin, Stella, and Janko. Back row second from the left; Stella's brother John Lloyd-Phillips.

and had many different faces. This, however, left the danger of betrayal no less prevalent. A Catholic priest, Fr. Heinrich Maier, was the leading figure in the Austrian resistance movement. He was eventually captured, and transported to Mauthausen. He was systematically tortured, crucified to a window frame, and later beheaded in Vienna in March 1945. His last words were: "Long live Christ, the King! Long live Austria!" Janko Musulin was exposed to this type of barbarity as

Fr. Heinrich Maier's police photograph

Janko Musulin presents his book programme on Austrian TV.
He was a director of the distinguished publishing house Fisher Verlag.

an enemy of the Third Reich. His name was on a list circulated after the July Plot against Hitler. The list named those considered capable of taking power in Austria should the plot have succeeded.

Stella and Janko were very compatible on many fronts. They came from similar social backgrounds, had shared intellectual interests, and had a strong sense of the need to fight the injustices they saw around them. This was not simply youthful enthusiasm; it was a view firmly held and one maintained and acted upon their entire lives. Both came from well-off backgrounds and had very little interest in money. This may have surprised his maternal grandfather, Baron Rudolph von Isbary, a wealthy industrialist.

It was he who acquired Schloss Fridau in 1913. Stella enjoyed telling the history of the castle. The baroque castle was built on the site of an earlier house which dated from 1299. In 1755 the present house was built by Johann Georg von Grechtler. Baroness Antonia (Antonietta) von Waldstätten inherited the estate in 1788. On her marriage to the Prince of Corsini, the property passed to that family. There were

Fähnrich Hellfried Freiherr von Isbary, geb. 5. Nov. 1893,
gefallen 17. Juli 1915.

Janko Musulin's great-uncle

two more owners, a Trauttmansdorff-Weinsberg count and
a Liechtenstein prince before it became the property of Stella's mother-in-law Else von Isbary and ultimately passed into the von Musulin family. The castle was bought in 1974 by
the government of Lower Austria. Stella and Janko used to
joke that the castle "represented the decline of the Gotha."

The couple married in Mariazell, just over an hour's drive
from Fridau. It is an ancient site of Marian pilgrimage where
a statue of the Virgin Mary, brought there in the twelfth century, is believed by the faithful to work miracles. A narrow-
gauge rail line allows the Mariazellerbahn to access the town
from the Lower Austrian state capital St. Pölten. This was
particularly convenient for the wedding party when petrol

The Musulin's house at Zell am See

Schloss Brandhof in Mariazell

rationing was still in place. The wedding reception proved to be quite a difficult event to organise. In 1946 post-war rationing was still very much in place in Austria. The country did not benefit from the Marshall Plan until 1948. Food riots occasionally raged in Vienna and the Communists were calling for a halt to the "westernisation" of Austrian politics. Against this background, Stella and her mother-in-law struggled to assemble a frugal wedding reception in Mariazell. Stella recalled her mother-in-law calling in all sorts of favours from friends to gather together enough dried fruits for a wedding cake.

Stella first came to Austria in 1936 on holiday to Brandhof at the suggestion of her half-sister Sonja. In 1937 she returned to stay again when she met many of the Austrian aristocrats who became her friends. It was here also that she first met Janko Musulin. The following year she became involved in the secret and dangerous world of espionage. She remained silent about those days and abided by the oath she swore when she signed the Official Secrets Act. Even her son Marko had no knowledge of this side of her life until after her death. Her recruitment into the hush-hush world of British Intelligence was done in London in 1938.

Of the many agents operating in Vienna, at the time of Stella's recruitment in London, Thomas Kendrick was one of Britain's top agents in the city between the wars. Though he is hardly a household name even today, he was responsible for saving an estimated ten thousand Austrian Jewish lives and for infiltrating the Comintern's organisation in the Austrian capital. Kim Philby worked for him at one time. He is also believed to have recruited the mother of Princess Michael of Kent, Hungarian Countess Marianne Szapáry. Undercover, as an official at the Passport Office, Kendrick, against the advice of London, was issuing documents to Jews in vast num-

Thomas Kendrick, Britain's chief spy in Vienna

bers. He was responsible for saving the lives of George Wei-denfeld and Jeremy Thorpe's future wife, Marion Stein. Stella became one of his replacements in the Passport Office building at Metternichgasse 6. She told Philip Mansel: "By day I issued passports, by night I danced." Her role was, of course, somewhat more substantial than that. She, too, like Kendrick, became involved in issuing passports to Jews. There had been a suggestion from within MI6 that she go undercover in Copenhagen once the German's intention to occupy Denmark became clear. However, it came to nothing as it was felt her training had been insufficient and she was sent to Vienna.

Once Stella had married, her days in espionage were essentially over. Her son Marko was born at her family's house, Dale Castle, in Pembrokeshire in 1948. Her father, Rhodri Vaughan Lloyd-Phillips, was Lord of the Manor of Dale. He inherited the estate in 1888. After he came down from Trinity College Cambridge, he spent time at Dale but later entered the British Army and was commissioned into the Life Guards. He fought in the South African War in 1899, where he saw action at the Relief of Kimberley, the Battle of Paarde-

Main entrance to Metternichgasse 6, home of the British Legation in Vienna where Stella worked. The rather grandly turned out Majordomo guarding the entrance in full regalia.

berg and the Battle of Colesberg in 1901. He was mentioned in dispatches several times and had six clasps to his Queen's Medal. He was appointed Lieutenant Colonel of the Royal Garrison Artillery in Gibraltar, where he served until the Great War ended. Stella's brother John followed his father into the British Army. He was educated at Stowe and Trinity College Cambridge and was commissioned into the Welsh Guards in 1942. During the war, he served in Algeria, Italy, and Austria and saw action at the battles of Monte Cerabola and Monte Cassino.

Life at Dale when Stella was born was typical of that enjoyed by the pre-war landed gentry. Plenty of indoor and outdoor servants were employed, including a chauffeur, a cook, and a nanny. A French Governess was employed to educate the young Stella. However, she resisted the rather pushy governess and insisted on being sent to Malvern Girls' College in Worcestershire at the age of eleven. It was an interesting choice because the school was not known particularly for its academic achievements but rather for producing "good citizens." Princess Alice, Duchess of Gloucester, attended the school as Lady Mary Montagu Douglas Scott, as did Barbara Cartland. The American World War II correspondent Tania Long was there at the same time as Stella and, like Stella, worked as a spy but for the precursor of the CIA. Another contemporary was the irrepressible Margaret Hampshire, who became principal of one of England's grandest

Stella and her son Marko at Zell am See

Dale Castle in Pembrokeshire. Stella's family home

Malvern Girls' College. Stella's old school.

girls' schools, Cheltenham Ladies' College. A former pupil described her as "a battleship in full sail—she had tremendous frontage."

Stella maintained close friendships with a handful of people she treasured throughout her life. One of her closest female friends was the English historian Lavender Goddard Wilson. Born Lavender Cassels, she was a friend of Freya Stark, whom she met in Benghazi, where her husband was secretary to the British Resident after the Allied occupation of Libya in 1942. As Lavender Cassels, she wrote two well-received books, one on the Ottoman Empire and another on the Habsburgs. She was a guest at Stella's wedding. Her closest male friend was an English barrister, Peter Boydell, a head of chambers in the Inns of Court in London. A brilliant legal mind, he was also passionate about history.

However, her best friend was Edith Silbermann, a childhood friend of Paul Celan. She and Celan came from the same town, Czernowitz in Romania, now Chernivtsi in Ukraine. Her family helped Celan escape when the Romanian Fascists and the Nazis were deporting Jews from the town. Silbermann has left a fascinating posthumously published memoir of her friendship and life-long devotion to Celan and his writings.

Stella (left), Edith Silbermann (right), and her husband Kuby, a chess grandmaster

Stella was philosemitic. She and her husband counted many of Vienna's Jewish intellectuals among their closest friends, and they both did whatever they could to secure publishing contracts for Jewish scholars and helped out financially whenever they could. After visiting the Majdanek concentration and extermination camp in Poland, the history of the holocaust was much on my mind. I discussed this with Stella as well as her interest in the Jewish intellectual world. Stella began by saying that it was one of the great regrets of her life that, with a pedigree dating back to the year 800, she could not find "a drop of Jewish blood" in her lineage.

She had a particular affection for the works of Thomas Mann and was delighted that Auden had married his daughter, Erika, to save her from a terrible fate in Berlin and equally delighted that they never divorced. She spoke of the profound impact of fin-de-siècle Jewish writing on the evolution of Viennese literature in the twentieth century. She emphasised the special relationship between Jewish writers and Vienna and the long-standing tensions between the city and its Jewish intellectuals. This Stella explained as a particularly Viennese situation where disparate non-Viennese groups often found themselves, in her phrase, "strangely at home" in Vienna.

The American-born composer and broadcaster Eugene Hartzell was also a good friend. They broadcast together on Radio Austria International under the direction of David Hermges, a former BBC journalist who later ran the English Service at the ORF. Stella liked to introduce Eugene Hartzell's music to friends. Hermges and Hartzell used to tease Stella about her very English RP rendering of Austria, which she delivered as Auus-tri-ah.

By the time I met Stella in 1984, she had been diagnosed with Parkinson's disease, a condition she bore with great fortitude, resilience, and humour. I brought someone to see her

Composer Eugene Hartzell

at Fridau, who was in awe of her. To break the ice, the poor chap said: "I hope you don't mind me saying so, Baroness, but how you sit so reminds me of the Duchess of Westminster." Stella was perched elegantly on the edge of a sofa, one leg crossed over the other at the ankle. "Really, how fascinating," Stella answered. "Does she have Parkinson's as well?" We were all convulsed with laughter; the embarrassing moment had been skilfully passed over by Stella.

Staying with her at Fridau was a joy. The train from Vienna to St. Pölten, then change for the narrow gauged Mariazellerbahn to Ober-Grafendorf, and there to meet one with a cheery smile was Stella's loyal maid Erika. The short drive to Fridau Castle was spent in monosyllabic utterances in German. "For God's sake, Michael, don't speak to Erika in German, she'll get the wrong idea of you," Stella had warned me. At this stage, my German consisted mostly of Viennese dialect picked up in "all the wrong places" as Stella put it rather good-heartedly.

Before unpacking, I always made a beeline for Stella's rooms. The door was left ajar, and my hostess invariably greet-

Painting of Saint Sebastian in Stella's guest bedroom

ed me with: "Do tell me all the gossip from Vienna. Who's not speaking to whom? Have you seen Mimi, how are the Hartzells?" Then we would sit chatting about what books we were reading. Before dinner, I crossed the cobbled courtyard to a guest bedroom warmed in winter by a rather grand cream-tiled Baroque wood-burning stove topped with a splendid corona to aggrandise its otherwise functional presence. Over the bed hung a large canvas depicting the martyrdom of St. Sebastian, his emaciated body pierced with arrows was a grim reminder of the castle's occupation by the Soviet Army. The painting was saved together with some family silver by an elderly manservant.

Dinner was always in Stella's cosy kitchen. The fare, typical Austrian tafelspitz or Wiener schnitzel followed by apfelstrudel, washed down with generous quantities of local wine, often a crisp Grüner Veltliner. Auden had dined at the same table in company with Chester, Stella's mother-in-law, and whosoever might be visiting. A whiskey and Turkish coffee after dinner then early to bed; the room was scented by the all-pervasive smell of pinewood from the stove.

Walks in the afternoon through the park where some ancient trees had escaped the excesses of the Soviet army's axes, were a leisurely affair. Occasional examples of old garden statuary could be glimpsed peeping out from behind the undergrowth. We usually sat in front of an impressive eighteenth-century orangerie, now sadly neglected, its missing panes of glass glared in disproof of Bastiat's parable of the broken window. Stella sat me in the exact spot where she photographed her mother-in-law and Auden. "Are you having an osmotic moment of transference?" Stella asked. We had many such exchanges in those wonderful years of our friendship.

Shortly before her death, Stella suffered a fall which resulted in her breaking her hip. She was hospitalised in St. Pölten but never fully recovered. She died at home in Fridau, in the arms of her Croatian nurse, Eva, on the night of January 21, 1996. She had endured years of watching her body, as she put it, "let her down" while her mind remained as sharp as a pin. She accepted her lot with stoic reserve. Stella was laid to rest after a Catholic Mass—she had converted in 1948—in the von Musulin family plot in Ober-Grafendorf. It is not a great distance from where her friend W. H. Auden rests.

V

**Stella's Journals
and
Auden's Letters**

NOTE

I was first given access to the following letters by Auden and journals by Stella Musulin in 1984. Since then, her son Marko has made a generous gift of them to the Austrian Academy of Sciences, where they are now available online at https://amp.acdh.oeaw.ac.at. I have not edited out any material that may differ slightly or repeat material from my account above. Written and oral accounts often vary, and I have tried to strike a balance between the two. Auden scholars and interested readers will find a treasure trove of material available to them on the above website, skilfully edited by the dedicated team of scholars at the Austrian Centre for Digital Humanities and Cultural Heritage at the Academy in Vienna under the direction of Dr. Sandra Mayer. I have added an occasional footnote to the texts where readers may find additional information useful. I have left in Stella's repetitions in her text because they were written at different times and were never meant to form a continuous recollective narrative.

The Years in Austria

Half an hour from the outskirts of Vienna, an invisible thread bisects the motorway. It leads from the church which lies to the north, more accurately speaking from the churchyard, disregards entirely the traffic as it thunders to and from the capital, wriggles across a field to the south, and passes a small house, which was once a garage. Up a steep path, plum trees on one side and apple trees on the other, through a wicket gate, and now the thread, which has turned neither to right nor left, has reached its objective: a long, low house, more an extended workman's cottage.

Originally, the address was Hinterholz 6; later, the lane up from the village on the other side was renamed Auden-Strasse. This thread or unseen line joins the places where Auden prayed, sang (flat) and was buried, and the place where he lived, and to me, it is a tangible reality, unfailingly sensed at each frequent crossing. Partly it is because it was always from that direction that I arrived, being mistrustful of the narrow lane which lies along the top of the garden and leads into a wood where, in a small clearing, floored at times by sticky mud, the car can be turned. It seemed preferable, and anyway became a habit, to take the cart track through the field with its ruts, the depth of which left the undercarriage to slide along the plateau of coarse grass. And to leave the car by the garage and plod up through the orchard, accepting the risk of slithering off the path to the right. On walking through the wicket-gate next to the woodshed, there has been, from time to time and is today, the risk of being savaged by a wall-eyed dog; in earlier days, having to account for one's presence to Frau Emma.[1]

Past the vegetable patch, now the ground levels off, and the house stands before us. Left, at the foot of the outside staircase and below the window of his workroom, there are the white table and comfortable garden chairs with red cushions. Facing the caller, the green door with a bell, the sort which jangles when pulled. I seldom did so, feeling that its clamour spoke of altogether too much aggressive jocularity. Seeing the light through the sitting-room window, it was better to walk straight into the small entrance hall—coats hanging on the wall ahead, kitchen through the right-hand door, a clutter of books and papers on a nearby ledge and to shout. That heartwarming bellow from Wystan: "Ah!" and here is the familiar scene, we are enveloped in the unchanging fug. The shelves of records and the oversized record player on the left, the big, square dining table with its food-stained cloth. Centre back, the Austrian peasant cupboard containing drinks, sugar, salt, then the corner seat, the table with its cigarette burns and glass rings, and two armchairs—a *Sitzecke*.[2] To our right a tumble of assorted titles on an invisible surface; within a matter of days, Auden could make a new book look like a lending library reject: the content was all, the package irrelevant. Here lie, precarious-

---

1   Emma Eiermann, Auden's housekeeper, who died in 1967.
2   A corner seat.

ly balanced, collapsing, upended volumes of poetry, cookery books, Benson's Lucia novels,[3] *Akenfield*,[4] whodunnits, a new translation of the Bible. Over the years, the content of the heap varied but the overall appearance scarcely at all. And now the stove, country style, a white dome with round green tiles set in it, one of the glories of Austrian *Wohnkultur*.[5] How fortunate that the stove is irremovable, or it would be in Athens now, along with the cupboard and the original drawings of Stravinsky and Richard Strauss.[6] Books also lie along the top ledge of the corner seat, and a volume or two of the OED on the upright chairs by the dinner table, adjuncts to the *Times* crossword. Was it, I asked, essential to have the complete Oxford English Dictionary, all thirteen volumes of it, at each of one's residences? "Of course," said Auden, surprised at such a question.

So much was written during his lifetime about Auden's way of life in Kirchstetten: articles by capable journalists in the Sunday papers and in their weekly magazines, that any attempt at a personal memoir gives the writer the feeling that he is working all too well-trodden ground. It is not only that the scene is familiar. What can a friend write without lapsing into triviality and gossip, without calling down on his head the wrath of Wystan Auden himself, about whom, if we know nothing else, we realise the obsession that he had on the subject of personal privacy. Think for a moment of *Forewords and Afterwords*[7]: again and again he writes on these lines: Of Wag-

---

3   A series of comic novels by the writer E.F. Benson from the 1920s and 1930s.
4   *Akenfield: Portrait of an English Village* by Ronald Blythe (1969).
5   German: home décor (lit. culture of living).
6   Auden also had drawings of Elizabeth Bishop and E.M. Forster, and an original William Blake watercolour.
7   A collection of 46 essays Auden wrote on historical, literary, and religious subjects, published in 1973.

ner: "On principle, I object to biographies of artists, since I do not believe that knowledge of their private lives sheds any significant light upon their works."[8] And on Oscar Wilde: "Since knowledge of an artist's private life never throws any significant light upon his work, there is no justification for intruding upon his privacy."[9] Listening to Kurt Weill records one winter's evening in Chester's flat in the Eslarngasse,[10] I asked him whether he could account for it. Disappointingly, Chester only said that it was an obsession with Wystan, an individual phobia like any other. The only time that Auden ever came near to snapping at me was when he spoke once, affectionately, of Tolkien, saying that he was to speak or write about him. Was he, I asked, going to say anything at all about the man as the creator of the world of Tolkien, of the *Lord of the Rings*? He said "Certainly not! I shouldn't dream of saying anything about Tolkien himself." So that the predicament is understood: either we keep silent when asked to speak and write about Auden, which might seem a trifle portentous, not to say uncivil. Or else we run the dual risk of triviality or indiscretion. In the eyes of others who knew him better, there is probably a further risk, that of being coupled with the German mythical figure, the horseman who rode, as he supposed, over the frozen Lake of Constance, unaware that this was not the case at all, but he was being carried along above dark waters, knowing nothing of the treacherous depths beneath him.[11] So that my contribution can be no more than an attempt to show how Auden lived among the Austrians,

---

8 From the essay "The Greatest of Monsters," ibid.
9 From the essay "An Improbable Life," ibid.
10 A street in Vienna's Dannebergplatz district.
11 A reference to the ballad "Der Reiter und der Bodensee" [The rider and Lake Constance] written in 1826 by the German writer Gustav Schwab.

on what sort of terms he was with them, and perhaps to fill in one or two gaps in what is generally known.

I got to know Wystan and Chester through the daughter of Hugo von Hofmannsthal,[12] Christiane Zimmer,[13] who was a friend of Auden's in New York. Gerty von Hofmannsthal, widow of the poet, who died in 1929, owned Schloss Prielau at the northern tip of the lake of Zell-am-See in Salzburg province. She had been forced to sell when the Nazis overran Austria but had regained possession at about the turn of the fifties, and there she spent her summers until she died, filling the house with her friends, often like herself Anglo-Austrian émigrés—the writers, artists, and scholars who had lived and worked in Vienna during the twilight of that great explosion of talent which coincided with the decline and end of the Austro-Hungarian Empire. Raimund and Liz von Hoffmannsthal[14] were often there, with their children Arabella and Octavian. There was a constant coming and going between Prielau and the rehearsals and then the performances of the Salzburg Festival; it was a great meeting place for retired birds of paradise such as Lady Diana Cooper,[15] Ledebur,[16] and the dancer and choreographer Grete Wiesenthal.[17] Gradually, a well-worn track developed between Prielau

---

12 Hugo von Hofmannstahl (1874–1929), Austrian poet, dramatist, and essayist, and collaborator with Richard Strauss.

13 Christiane Zimmer (1902–1987), Austro-American social scientist and widow of the German Indologist Heinrich Zimmer (1890–1943).

14 Hugo von Hohmannsthal's son and his second wife, Lady Elizabeth Paget.

15 Lady Diana Cooper, Viscountess Norwich (1892–1986), English actress, aristocrat, and well-known social figure in the London and Paris scene.

16 Friedrich von Ledebur (1900–1986), Austrian-born actor most well-known for playing Queequeg in the 1956 version of Moby Dick.

17 Grete Wiesenthal (1885–1970), Austrian dancer, actor, choreographer, and dance teacher.

and our house at the upper end of the Schmittenhöhe val-
ley, and friendships grew between my family and the Hof-
mannsthals and several of their friends, which have survived
and have been continued by our children.

My marriage broke up during 1957–58 and my son Marko[18] and I went to live with my mother-in-law Elsa Musulin[19]
at her home Schloss Fridau, in Lower Austria, about half an
hour's drive from Kirchstetten. She will rate a mention here
because of the entertainment value she was to acquire for
Auden. It was in 1958 that by chance, I met Christiane Zimmer at Prielau, and she suggested I should call on Auden: "After all, he's your neighbour now." I demurred with some en-
ergy, having a great dislike of pursuing the famous except
in the way of business where an interview is called for. The
next time I saw her—in 1959—she asked whether I had seen
Auden, I again scoffed at the very idea that he might "love
to meet me," and she said "All right. I'm just off to spend
a week there now and I shall fix it." So in due course I came
to be standing at the green door, and yet the memory that
remains is the shock of Chester's appearance as he stood in
the doorway in the strong sunlight: pale, misshapen, fish-
eyed, loose-mouthed; it was the unpromising kind of exteri-
or which makes one impatient to discover what lies behind
it, the general impression however was one of anxious be-
nevolence, and this proved roughly correct. The second time
I was invited over to Kirchstetten was a more convivial occasion: Wystan had asked me to come over and stand by him because he was giving a little tea-party. He had invited the parish priest, Father Lustkandl—crystallized in "Whitsunday in

18 Dr. Marko Musulin (1948), Austrian lawyer and businessman, for-
    merly with Creditanstalt-Bankverein Wien.
19 Elsa Musulin neé Isbary (1889–1976).

Kirchstetten"[20]—the local school mistress Frau Seitz and her silent husband, and as I came in I ran into Auden who was shuffling out to the kitchen. "Thank goodness you've come," he hissed, "go and look after them, will you, keep the conversation going and hand round the cakes." Whereupon he shot into the kitchen for more hot water. It was some time before he could abandon the role of the flustered host. His guests were quite at their ease, and as the years went on they became his friends. Their composure that day was, I am sure, partly due to their own personal qualities, but partly, too, to the fact that in Josef Weinheber[21] they had had their local poet laureate before, and now they had one again. This was a cause for great satisfaction, but not for any transports of ecstasy over the celebrity in their midst.

What was so "American" about the "kitchen in Lower Austria?"[22] Nothing much, so far as I could see. When fitted kitchens first came in, Austrians dubbed them "American." The term is now as extinct as "Russian" tea, but must still have been common parlance in Kirchstetten when Wystan wrote the poem. There was a tidy row consisting of a fridge, sink, low cupboards with a good working surface, a corner cupboard the interior of which swung out, and a gas stove. Both men were very proud of the kitchen and it became Chester's habitat. But the whole point of a modern kitchen: the clear surfaces, ample storage space, accessibility, the careful rationalisation, was totally cancelled out by the permanent clutter which invaded the room at once and never left it. It was a mat-

---

20   Title of a 1965 poem by Auden and published in the collection *About the House* (1965).

21   Josef Weinheber (1892–1945), Austrian lyric poet, writer, and essayist much favoured by the Nazis. Weinheber committed suicide in 1945.

22   A reference to Auden's 1958 poem "On Installing an American Kitchen in Lower Austria," published in *Homage to Clio* (1960). The poem was later retitled "Grub First, Then Ethics."

ter of principle with Chester to have all cooking ingredients conveniently to hand, but this meant that nothing was ever put away, and where his loving eye saw method, even the least fussy visitor could only observe a shambles. But an interesting shambles, because of the exotic nature of the preserved foods and spices that Chester brought with him. From an early date I was convinced that they were both eating their way into their graves owing to the enormous fat content of some of the dishes. I remember the horror with which I watched a sauce being prepared in the mixer before being re-heated to accompany the roast duck. First, Chester poured in the rendered down fat from the baking tin, about half a pint of it, then he added an equal quantity of cream, a little seasoning, and switched on the mixer. The result would have sustained a miner at the coal face for a full working day, but neither Wystan nor Chester walked a yard if they could help it.

The small heap of correspondence lying on the filing cabinet beside my desk puts me in mind of the rise and fall of the telegram as a means of social communication. In English novels during the period up to and even well beyond the first world war—particularly in detective stories—the incessant despatch and receipt of telegrams, often of some length, play a prominent part in human relationships. They were an astonishingly rapid and comparatively inexpensive medium of communication and were often employed over short distances. In Austria, the reign of the telegram persisted into the sixties, lost ground sharply owing to automatisation, but enjoyed one last Indian summer in the post office at Kirchstetten. There was no telephone in the house because of the distance from the nearest point of contact; it would have been too expensive to install.

Also, Auden liked his peace and quiet and when he wanted to telephone he did so from the post office, combining [it] with his daily shopping expedition. The lack of a telephone accounts for much of my correspondence with Auden, or rather, because I have only scant records of what I wrote, for his letters to me, and especially for the telegrams. "We are here, where are you?" or "Wednesday would suit perfectly" and so on, are messages which mark the development of a cosy routine of coming and going between Schloss Fridau, my mother-in- law's place where I have a flat, and Kirchstetten. "Mama" was an eccentric of the old-fashioned kind to be met with in many countries. Auden recognised the type at once and rejoiced: a rough exterior and an abrupt manner, one who had feared neither Nazis nor Russian occupiers, obstinate, shy, cultured, not troubled by surface blemishes, hospitable, terrifyingly outspoken, and fond of good food. He liked to be asked out in any case, and Fridau is an easy 25 minutes' drive from Kirchstetten, as it were across the fields: not round by Böheimkirchen and St. Pölten, but across farmland and through villages, along lanes so winding that only a snake could have planned them.

He, too, liked his food, all the more so if it were roast saddle of roe deer with cranberry preserve, wild duck or roast pheasant, with a good wine, followed by one of the richer Austrian cakes—Wurmbrand-Torte, for instance, which consists mainly of ground burnt almonds and creamed chocolate—and then to carry one's wine glass back into the sitting room and wait while the Turkish coffee ceremony was performed. This was, down all the years that I have known Fridau, and still is, the indispensable conclusion to lunches even of the humbler, everyday sort: Turkish coffee with the *kaimak* hissing faintly as the cup is filled—that pale brown foam which must be removed as the coffee rises to the boil and carefully shared out between the empty cups. Failure to do this is the unforgivable sin. And Auden would sit, well nourished, blinking in the sunshine from the window opposite him from where he could see the crown of an immense pear tree. After his second cup he was likely to leap to his feet without any of those preliminary movements of eyes, hands, and feet with which people signal their imminent departure, shake hands all round and hurry away. But sometimes he felt like a turn round the park, or even to stay on for a time, sitting in a deck chair under the trees in the courtyard. But if he hurried, it was no discourtesy; Wystan was the most courteous of men, who liked to follow the customs of the country he lived in, and above all he had no special voice for employees. He got on well with Austrian people who sometimes—without the natural excuse of his food storekeeper in St. Mark's Place—had no idea of the calibre of the man with whom, in his home or theirs, they were having a meal. As I knew him, the only thing he couldn't bear was pretension. So one would have supposed that writers young and older would have lost no time in beating a path out to Kirchstetten.

Are writers convivial creatures? Do they like to congregate together for mutual admiration and to complain about their publishers? At some times and in some places, yes, at others no; that they have the patience to listen to each other reading their works aloud is true, probably, only in circumstances of political persecution. Be it as it may, I sometimes see Auden's relationship with the literary scene in Austria—such as it is—as a string of wasted opportunities. He was interviewed, he was filmed, and the Gesellschaft für Literatur[23] did its duty by him and more, from start to finish. It still does. But the Austrian Society for Literature is neither

---

23 Österreichische Gesellschaft für Literatur (Austrian Society for Literature), founded in 1961 by the Austrian Ministry of Education.

a club nor a coffee house, but a society for the promotion of literature, with a particular mission to writers in communist Eastern Europe. Somehow, in the sixties, there was otherwise no group of people, no meeting place towards which Auden himself could naturally gravitate. Think of this in terms of the old pre-war Vienna, the life in the coffee houses where the literary figures of the earlier twentieth century congregated, where they spent their days, read their correspondence and the newspapers, read and wrote criticisms, blacked each other's characters: the Café Central[24] and the Herrenhof.[25] I can imagine Auden in this atmosphere very well, enjoying the opportunity it gave him of rubbing shoulders with writers of all ages, and particularly with the young, as it were by chance, without further commitment on either side and with the minimum of effort. I can see the cigarette ash on the marble topped tables, the mounds of paper, see Auden slopping to and fro in his eternal bedroom slippers between his table and the telephone kiosk. But this world ended when Egon Friedell,[26] giving the passers by a shout of warning as he did so, jumped out of the window to his death on the entry of the Nazis. It was a world, described again and again by those who knew it, never more effectively than by one of its last active, working survivors, Friedrich Torberg,[27] and it has gone for ever. Today's writers have no time. They are dash-

---

24 Café Central, opened in 1876 and subsequently a popular meeting place for Viennese and émigré intellectuals of the late nineteenth and early twentieth centuries.

25 Café Herrenhof, opened in 1914, an important literary café of the interwar period. Café Herrenhof closed in 2006.

26 Egon Friedell (1878–1938) was a prominent Austrian cultural historian, actor, playwright, essayist, and cabaret performer.

27 Friedrich Torberg, pen-name of Friedrich Kantor (1908–1979), Austrian writer and anti-Nazi journalist who worked in Hollywood before returning to Vienna in 1951.

ing from recording studios beyond Schönbrunn[28] to newspaper offices at the opposite end of Vienna, from the head
post office to their homes, where they kiss wife and children,
snatch a bag and rush to the airport or to a railway terminal.
Alternatively, like Thomas Bernhard,[29] they bury themselves
in a farmhouse in a district carefully chosen for its unfash-
ionableness and difficulty of access, emerging, like cats, only on their own terms, preferring to turn up unannounced
in their friends' houses, perhaps late at night, enquiring for
just that ration of warmth, light, and unquestioning accep-
tance which, at that moment, they happen to need. Bernhard's fame has now altered the character of the district he
lives in and he has withdrawn to still more distant quarters.

Auden always wanted to meet Bernhard, and asked me to
mediate, which I did on several occasions, but to no effect;
I think I did overcome Bernhard's disinclination but the moment never arrived. The cultural historian Friedrich Heer,[30]
on the other hand, asked whether he would like to go out
to lunch in Kirchstetten, replied that he would go—he has
a tendency towards hyperbole—"on my knees." The day is
described in a letter of mine to a friend in Germany, dated
29th May ... "I still can't put yesterday's expedition to Kirchstetten out of my mind. Fritz Heer and I drove out to lunch.
This manic-depressive genius Friedrich Heer, *dieser verschreckte
Lausbub*,[31] and the great English poet Auden—to say nothing

---

28 Schönbrunn Palace, the main summer residence of the Habsburg
    rulers, located in Hietzing, Vienna.
29 Thomas Bernhard (1931–1989), Austrian novelist, playwright, and
    poet noted for his focus on pessimistic topics such as death, social in-
    justice, and human misery.
30 Friedrich Heer (1916–1983), Austrian historian and founder of an
    anti-Nazi Catholic resistance group during the war.
31 German: "this terrified rascal"; it is possible this was a failed attempt
    on Musulin's part to render *l'enfant terrible* into German.

of Kallman—how would it go off? It went like a bomb. Fritz
was like a man let out of prison. For months at a time he never escapes from the treadmill and he rejoiced so over the soft
greens of the Vienna Woods, over the acacia trees whose silver
shimmer stood out against the darker background, over the
good air, the clear view after the storm of two days ago. I was
a bit worried that the two big talkers might both speak at once
or at cross purposes, but this only happened occasionally:
each really wanted to hear what the other had to say, they ex-
changed anecdotes and sometimes they moved on to ground
where Chester and I couldn't follow them. Each picked up the
other's illusions instantly, and the *Stimmung*[32] was wonderful.
We were on one of my favourite hobby-horses, the destruction of the German language by the Nazis. But Fritz insisted
that Mussolini had vulgarized Italian in the same way, and
suddenly he drew himself up, threw out his chest, his face
became a live mask of Mussolini and he held forth in Italian
in a ranting, hectoring, high-pitched tone—a performance
which could have been transferred to any cabaret unaltered.
I never knew he had such a talent for mimicry. Nor was this
all. The conversation moved to France and the Paris intellectuals, and now Fritz topped up his cabaret with a simpering,
lovingly luxuriant interchange between Gide[33] and Claudel.[34]
Wystan was convulsed. The talk shifted to Wagner's texts, liturgical reform, Weinheber, Rudolf Kassner[35] and Freud; of
these three Fritz could speak from personal knowledge. Unless Auden had friends to stay, talk of this quality was a rare

32 German: mood; atmosphere.
33 André Gide (1869–1951), French writer, humanist, and moralist,
    winner of the 1947 Nobel Prize for Literature.
34 Paul Claudel (1868–1955), French poet, dramatist, and diplomat not-
    ed for his devout Catholicism.
35 Rudolf Kassner (1873–1959), Austrian writer, essayist, and cultural
    philosopher; noted for his translations of the poet William Blake.

occurrence. It was possible to see why Bernhard, to take one example, did not care to go to Kirchstetten: there was a kind of gène,[36] and a quite unjustified fear that he would have to speak English. But it is impossible to discern any reason, apart from lack of time, which could have got in the way of personal contact between Auden and his translators.

During his early years in Kirchstetten Auden did feel slighted by some of his translators in Austria and Germany who would publish their work in literary magazines, and if the poet himself ever heard of it, it was by pure chance. "They don't," he said indignantly, "even send me a copy of their paper." Nor, in those days, was he satisfied with the quality of the work. He said to an interviewer in Berlin, at a time when little of his poetry had been translated into German: "Translating poetry into a different language is very, very problematical—and apart from that, people earn too little by it." But: "Why can't one send the translation to a living poet before it is published?" He might not know the exactly suitable word, but he would know what image a word or a phrase was intended to call up in the reader. "For instance, I spoke in a poem about corn—maize—but the translator rendered it as wheat! I was annoyed, because that sort of thing can be avoided." The fifty-minute drive to Kirchstetten presented too great a psychological barrier even to the young, now dead, author and poet Gerhard Fritsch[37] (he committed suicide) who translated Auden's Christmas Oratorio "For the Time Being"[38] into German. It was published

---

36 French: discomfort; embarrassment.

37 Gerhard Fritsch (1924–1969), Austrian poet and novelist who published two well-received novels, *Moos auf den Steinen* (Moss on the stones) and *Fasching* (Carnival).

38 Auden's "For the Time Being: A Christmas Oratorio" was written in 1941–42 and first published in the collection *For the Time Being* (1944).

in 1961 under the title "Hier und Jetzt" (Here and now). The translation is no masterpiece, but it was an attempt to demonstrate a style of writing which has always been very English and is characteristic of Auden even within the confines of a stanza: shifts in tone from the lofty to the colloquial. In "For the Time Being" Auden's language can be surrealistic, every-day, ironical, grotesque, mocking, tender, full of grief, rising to moments of lyrical joy. Rarely even attempted in German literature, in religious writing tone changes of this description are unknown. Austrian television showed a version of the oratorio on the eve of Epiphany—January 5, 1967—in which the libretto article in *Die Zeit*, Hamburg, April 23, 1965, by Cornelia Jacobsen,[39] was adapted and the music written by the composer Paul Kont.[40] A review by the critic Helmut A. Fiechtner[41] in "Die Furche" (The Furrow) gives the impression that it was a performance which, like Victorian children, should be seen but not heard. Design and costumes were by one of Austria's leading painters of the postwar era, Anton Lehmden,[42] singers of the calibre of Gloria Davy[43] and Hilde Rössel-Majdan[44] did their best, but the music was unconvincing, it got in the way of the text, and the

---

39 Cornelia Schmalz-Jacobsen (1934), German journalist and former general-secretary of the Free Democratic Party (FDP).

40 Paul Kont (1920–2000), Austrian composer, musical educator, and conductor. The musical rendition of Auden's "For the Time Being" was entitled *Inzwischen* (Meanwhile).

41 Dr. Helmut A. Fiechtner (1911–1984), Romanian-Austrian composer, journalist, and music critic; noted also for a biography of Hugo von Hofmannstahl.

42 Anton Lehmden (1929–2018), Austrian painter and printer of the Austrian School of Fantastic Realism.

43 Gloria Davy (1931–2012), American-Swiss soprano noted for her interpretations of Richard Strauss, Benjamin Britten and Paul Hindemith.

44 Hilde Rössel-Majdan (1921–2010), Austrian contralto of both opera and early baroque concert performances and recordings.

most impressive passage, not surprisingly, was Helmut Qualtinger's[45] monologue as Herod. In the following year, there
was a reading of "Hier und Jetzt" in the Palais Pálffy[46] under
the auspices of the Society for Literature. Auden read a short
passage in English and an actor took over and read in German. It appears that Auden was not satisfied, as he kept muttering "Nonsense—completely wrong!" and making notes in
the margin. In later years things changed very much for the
better, and although Auden did not actually live to see the
volume *Gedichte—Poems* published in English and German in
Vienna in 1973,[47] he did check the proofs, and a few of the
translators had been to see him. Today, more of Auden's poetry exists in German than in any other foreign language.

* * *

Talking of translations: whatever became of the Ford Foundation translation scheme? At one time Auden was thinking
about a plan in which he had become involved. This was to
bring all the main literary works in the German language
under review in so far as they exist in English translation, to
judge their quality and to discover the gaps. The real purpose
of the exercise was one with which Auden wholly agreed: to
encourage professional writers of the first category to take
part in the re-creation of German literature in English. To
this end the Ford Foundation would make funds available.
Even at that time, for a publisher to have native poetry on his

---

45 Helmut Qualtinger (1928–1986), Austrian actor, reciter, and cabaret
    performer, best known for his role in *The Name of the Rose*.
46 Palais Pálffy is a former palace of the Pálffy family located in Vien-
    na's Innere Stadt and now used primarily as a concert venue.
47 W. H. Auden, *Gedichte/Poems,* trans. Ernst Jandl et al. (Vienna: Eu-
    ropaverlag, 1973).

lists showed idealism enough. A translation fee usually wiped out any conceivable profits on literary prose texts or poetry. Nothing, of course, came of the scheme. Why, I don't know; we had a lot of fun making lists on the backs of envelopes and lamenting the impossibility of sharing playwrights like Raimund,[48] Nestroy[49] and Grillparzer[50] and novelists like Adalbert Stifter[51] with the English-speaking world. Auden knew quite well, of course, that it is not so much the language barrier, as a fatal lack of universality which has made so many leading Austrian writers—as used to be said of Austrian wine though with less justification—travel so badly.

In a foreword to a book I wrote on Austria[52] Auden was to write: "The relation between Art and Society is so obscure that only a fool will claim that he understands it. How, as the author asks in her concluding chapter on Vienna, is one to explain the extraordinary eruption of genius in that city which began during the last decades of the nineteenth century and lasted until the late 1920s, manifesting itself in every field, literature, music, painting, philosophy, medicine? When it began the empire was already dying on its feet, and it continued after its total collapse. Why? Even more extraor-

---

48 Ferdinand Raimund (1790–1836), Austrian actor, dramatist, and master of the Viennese farce. His plays *Bauer als Millionär* (1826), *Der Alpenkönig und der Menschenfeind* (1828) and *Der Verschwender* (1834) are still popular today.

49 Johann Nestroy (1801–1862), Austrian singer, actor, and playwright of the Biedermeier period. His musical play *Einen Jux will er sich machen* (1842) served as the basis for the 1964 musical *Hello Dolly!*

50 Franz Grillparzer (1791–1872), Austria's leading dramatist of the nineteenth century, best known for his plays *Medea* (1821), *Der Traum ein Leben* (1834), and *Die Jüdin von Toledo* (1851).

51 Adalbert Stifter (1805–1868), Austrian writer, painter, poet, and pedagogue. His novel *Der Nachsommer* (1857) is considered one of the finest examples of Bildungsroman.

52 Stella Musulin, *Austria: People and Landscape* (London: Faber & Faber, 1971).

dinary in my opinion were the artistic achievements of men like Nestroy and Adalbert Stifter living in Metternich's police state. More than that, I cannot help wondering if they could have written what they did under a more liberal regime. Talking of Stifter, (the author) says that he, like the composer Bruckner, 'has not travelled well.' Of Bruckner this may be true, but of Stifter I would say that he has not travelled, period: until a few years ago nobody had attempted to translate him."

Perhaps it is worth reminding ourselves of the abortive scheme in these difficult times, because of the underlying principle: that leading writers of the day, who can no doubt earn good money in other ways, should be given some form of inducement to translate from foreign languages at a standard equivalent to the original. And also, to recall that Auden himself was a translator of great stature. On the whole, it is arguable that English literature has been better served by its German translators than vice versa. The excellence of Rudolf Alexander Schröder's[53] version of T.S. Eliot's *Murder in the Cathedral* comes to mind: a major writer himself, Schröder produced a rendering in which all the cadences, the true Eliot "sound" are there, so that it is almost a matter of indifference whether the play is read in English or German. And in a way, Eliot hardly deserved it: Not long ago George Steiner[54] referred to English writers' lack of a sympathy towards the German classics and mentioned Auden as a striking exception. Leaving Shakespeare on one side, as no modern transla-

---

53 Rudolf Alexander Schröder (1878–1962), German poet and translator known for his translations of Homer, Horace, Virgil, Corneille, Racine, Molière, Shakespeare, and T. S. Eliot; Schröder was nominated five times for the Nobel Prize.

54 George Steiner (1929–2020), Franco-American literary critic, essayist, philosopher, novelist, and educator.

tors have managed to banish the Schlegel-Tieck version from the stage, Eva Hesse[55] made her name with Ezra Pound's *The Cantos*,[56] a masterpiece of the translator's art.

Auden immensely enjoyed working on Goethe's *Italian Journey*, and was always delighted when he came upon errors in the original caused by Goethe's own faulty editing. Goethe as a man fascinated him—three items in *Forewords and Afterwords* and much else of an earlier date are there to prove it. So it can't have been later than 1962 when there was a ring at the doorbell of my flat in Vienna. I opened the door and there was Auden, panting, as well he might because this was before our lift was put in and he had climbed ninety steps from street level. His shirt was grubby, his tie askew, his hair was matted, and before he was half through the door and with no further greeting he gasped out: "I have come to the conclusion that Goethe was a very lonely man." Which I think we may doubt. But Auden knew loneliness.

> Gate-crashing ghost, aggressive
> invisible visitor,
> tactless gooseberry, spoiling
> my tête-à-tête with myself,
> blackmailing brute, behaving
> as if the house were your own...

The strength, the violence of the pictures in this poem can hardly be paralleled in any other on a related subject. Loneliness is a vicious being, which makes the mind a quagmire of disquiet. A shadow without shape or sex, excluding con-

---

55 Eva Hesse (1925–2020), one of Germany's most distinguished translators and acute critics of Anglo-American literary modernism.
56 Ezra Pound, *22 Versuche über einen Dichter*, ed. Eva Hesse (Frankfurt am Main: Athenaum Verlag, 1967).

solation, blotting out Nature's beauties, it is a grey mist between the self and God. What helps? Routine; typing business letters. But Auden is safe from its haunting only when
fast asleep. Yet: tomorrow

> *Chester, my chum, will return.*
> *Then you'll be through: in no time*
> *he'll throw you out neck-and-crop,*
> *We'll merry-make your cadence*
> *with music, feasting and fun.*[57]

When Auden walked into Neulinggasse 26[58] and said what
he did about Goethe, it would be almost nine years before
he would write this poem, but he was already facing what
may have seemed the disaster of Chester's decision not to return to New York.

In October 1964 he went to a PEN conference in Budapest, and came back saying that he had heard an unbeliev-
able amount of hot air. The French delegates had got on his
nerves with much talk about "mon âme."[59] He may have been
unjust; Auden was not a lover of the French language, and
said that it is quite wrong to call it the most precise and logical of languages; in no other can a person deliver himself
of so much intellectual gibberish. But I had the courage to
remind him that Paul Tillich[60] had said he had learned to
think by having to express himself in English and to teach
Orientals in that language. When he read what he had writ-

---

57 From the poem "Loneliness," first published in *The Atlantic* in 1971 and
    later in the collection *Epistle to a Godson* in 1972.
58 The address of Stella's Vienna flat.
59 French: my soul.
60 Paul Tillich (1886–1965), German-American Christian existentialist
    philosopher, religious socialist, and Lutheran theologian.

ten years before in German he could barely understand it. By the end of October 1964 Auden was in Berlin, where he would spend the winter as a guest of the Ford Foundation. As a visiting professor he would give lectures and be at the disposal of students who wanted to consult him. On 21st November he was arrested for drunk driving. It must have been rather a dreary Christmas, and he remarked in a letter that he was lonely, as who wouldn't be in the circumstances.

Berlin-Dahlem,
Hubertusbaderstrasse 43
Deutschland

23rd December, 1964:
"It was sweet of you to think of me at Christmas, especially since it's a little *einsam*[61] here. Am beginning to know some local inhabitants. Oddly enough, the ones I can talk to most easily are from Ost-Berlin. The most awful thing about the *Bifkes*[62] (sic) is that they are so much nicer under a little *Druck*. When they feel their oats they are so apt to become uppish."

This was the private Auden. The public Auden in the interview with *Die Zeit* quoted earlier, hotly denied that he had been lonely. Many of his predecessors, said the interviewer, had repeatedly complained that little notice had been taken of them and that their stay was far from enjoyable. Auden's reply was "brusque": Grumbles of that sort were, he thought, unfair and personally objectionable. "One always has to do something to establish contacts, no one can do that for one." Not even the

---

61 German: lonely; lonesome.
62 German: A misspelling of the word *Piefke*, an Austrian derogatory term for Germans from the former Prussian states.

wealthy Ford Foundation or the Berlin senate. It was very un-
grateful to accept a monthly grant of a couple of thousand
marks and then to start criticising, instead of being thank-
ful to be free to work without financial worries—how often
was this possible? He himself, he went on, was extraordinarily glad that in Berlin, if that was what a person wanted, he was
left in peace; he was used to this "live and let live" in New York.

Characteristic though it is, one might not feel justified
in quoting from this letter if it were not for the fact that it
goes on to throw light on a passage in his long poem to Josef Weinheber. It came about like this: I had been reading
a paperback called *The Rise of the South African Reich* by Brian
Bunting and mentioned it in my letter with particular reference to torture. And I had complained that certain attitudes
found in so-called liberal circles tended to push one further
to the right than one wished to go. After a sharp comment
on the American magazine 'The National Review' he continues: 'Of course you're right about the lib-labs' ostrich attitude
to those who wish to destroy them, but one cannot let ones
name be associated with shits. Torture is the iniquity which
utterly bewilders me. I know something about the evil in my
own heart and in the sort of people I meet, but I cannot con-
ceive of myself or them torturing anybody. Where do the torturers come from? What class? Whom do they marry?' The
words 'Have you ever met one?' are deleted. 'To what pubs
do they go? Much love and best wishes for 1965, Wystan.' By
20th March 1965 he had completed, typed out and sent off to
me the long poem to Weinheber, with the verse:

Today we smile at weddings
Where bride and bridegroom
Were both born since the Shadow
Lifted, or rather

Moved elsewhere. Never as yet
Has Earth been without
Her bad patch, some unplace with
Jobs for torturers.
(In what bars are they welcome?
What girls marry them?)[63]

Later on, I told Chester about this infinitesimal and un-
witting contribution of mine to English literature. Chester
snapped: "Wystan never wastes anything." There exists a prose
translation of the poem to Weinheber, made by Auden and
"a German friend," which he sent to me for checking together
with some amendments to stanza three. As the occasion for
which the poem was written was a celebration of the twentieth anniversary of Weinheber's death, the prose translation
was for general information. "Herewith my effort," Auden
wrote, "to do my *Gemeindepflicht*." (his civic duty.) It hardly
needs saying that Auden's interest in Weinheber went far beyond a mere civic duty. It was part of his whole relationship
with Lower Austria, his feeling for the landscape, for its history, for the history of the people who lived, or had lived
there. For some reason he felt at home there, and the truth
of this is to be found in the best known poems of his last decade—perhaps they are among the best he ever wrote. There
is the first part of "The Cave of Making" (In Memoriam Louis
MacNeice.)[64] He often emphasizes how unsensational it all is:

"In a house backed by orderly woods,
    Facing a tractored sugar-beet country,

---

63 From the poem "Joseph Weinheber," first published in *London Maga-
    zine* in July 1965 and later in the collection *About the House*, also in 1965.
64 From the collection *About the House* published in 1965, which cele-
    brates his Kirchstetten Eden.

Your working hosts engaged to their stint,
You are unlike to encounter
Dragons or romance: were drama a craving,
You would not have come."

"For Friends Only" (for John and Teckla Clark).[65]

It strikes me suddenly as odd that he should have said
that: in the mythology of Austria this area is not, I believe,
dragon country.

Or in "The Common Life" (for Chester Kallman):[66]

I'm glad the builder gave
our common-room small windows
through which no observer outside can observe us:

Quite untrue. If they had the light on, anyone approach-
ing the door could and did see them. In the poem to Weinheber he tells him: "Here, though, I feel as at home as you did."
But the most moving declaration is in "Prologue at Sixty" (for
Friedrich Heer).[67] It satisfied him to live next door to where
the poet Josef Weinheber had lived, a man for whom he felt
a remarkable empathy and a strange compassion. It has occurred to me that an element in this sense of identity might
have been this: that he himself had once changed his mind.
He, like Weinheber, had made a political error and had entirely turned away from it. Weinheber had allowed himself
to be wooed by the Nazis, but later on he rejected it all and

---

65 Ibid.
66 Ibid.
67 First published in the May 1967 issue of *New York Review* and later in
    the collection *City without Walls* (1969).

finally he committed suicide. This may be fanciful; it is put forward simply as a suggestion. Auden knew that he would have got on with the man next door.

> Categorised enemies
> twenty years ago,
> now next-door neighbours, we might
> have become good friends,
> sharing a common ambit
> and love of the Word,
> over a golden *Kremser*
> had many a long
> language on syntax, commas, versification.[68]

On May 24th 1965, under the auspices of the Austro-British Council and the Society for Literature, Auden gave a talk on T.S. Eliot in the lecture hall of the Natural History Museum on the Ring.[69] It was very well attended, largely by crowds of note-taking students of Eng. Lit, and I have never been quite sure whether, at one moment, he was treating us to a bit of traditional stage business. He told us that there is a game: if, like the Trinity, we were made up of three persons, what would they be? Eliot, now, contained, firstly, the American pre-Jackson aristocrat of a kind which died out in 1829. He was a dandy, very carefully dressed in black jacket, striped trousers and bowler hat. And he worked two floors underground. Then there was the little boy aged twelve, adoring practical jokes such as cushions which fart when you sit on them, and who liked to shock people by saying "Goethe is awful" and so on. Finally, there

---

68 From "Joseph Weinheber," ibid.
69 Vienna's Ringstrasse.

was the Yiddish Momma... At this point a cascade of papers fell off the high reading desk. Auden disappeared altogether from our sight, scuffed about on the floor for a bit and finally emerged, very slowly, to complete his sentence: "... who wrote the poems." By now a very few people were shaking with silent laughter, but the students, with poised biros, blank-faced and puzzled, were waiting for all this to stop. He was understandably proud of having been asked to preach in Westminster Abbey.[70] His triumphant comment to me was: "Eliot never did that."

April 1967 brought a literary congress on avantgarde literature to the Palais Pálffy on the Josefsplatz in Vienna. Auden came, together with a rich, at moments over-rich collection of dons, writers, and critics from eastern and western Europe. A number of journalists and a few public figures were present by invitation, but no intervention from the floor was allowed and seldom desired by the listeners. It was enough to hear François Bondy[71] and Mary McCarthy,[72] to enjoy the striking contrast between Yefrim Etkind[73] of Leningrad and the square-headed commissar type from Moscow. And if some of the read contributions were dry, lifeless and badly delivered, we only had to wait for the knockout blow from Mar-

---

70 Auden preached at the Abbey on October 18, 1966 during the Abbey's ninth centenary.

71 François Bondy (1915–2003), Swiss journalist, translator, and novelist, former editor-in-chief of the French political and cultural magazine *Preuves*.

72 Mary McCarthy (1912–1989), American novelist, critic, and political activist, best known for her novel *The Group*. McCarthy was also once married to the American writer, literary critic and journalist Edmund Wilson.

73 Yefim Etkind (1918–1999) Soviet philologist, literary historian, and translation theorist; Etkind was expelled in 1974 and took up residence in France.

cel Reich-Ranicki[74] On the whole it was this leading West German critic with his maddeningly declamatory style and wagging index finger who dominated the platform, but it was Etkind who with his quiet, reasonable argument and his good manners won the affection of everyone in the room. A face-the-public session in the Redoutensaal[75] on the other side of the Josefsplatz ended the congress. I asked Auden whether there was anything I could do to help such as lending him my flat, and he promptly replied: "Yes, help me to look after Philip and Mary."

We agreed that we would all meet for supper in the Neulinggasse after the public session. Since I have no pretensions to being a literary hostess, I found the prospect alarming. It was not that, as a journalist, famous men worried me in the least, but famous women are somehow a different matter and I was inclined to be overawed by Mary McCarthy. But Chester was reassuring. "Don't you worry about Mary, she won't eat you. In fact she'll be charming, she'll merely put you in her next book."

A hostess should be at home to welcome her guests, or at the very least, she should arrive with them. I did neither. Having allowed myself to be pushed down towards the front of the hall, I was trapped and unable to get out, whereas the members of the congress left the platform and were free. I at last fought my way out and the search began for Yefrim Etkind whom I had invited as an eastern foil for the westerners He was run to ground in a back passage, surrounded by fans. It was only

---

74 Marcel Reich-Ranicki (1920–2013), leading German literary critic, member of the Gruppe 47 literary association, and survivor of the Warsaw Ghetto.

75 One of two former ballrooms (Grosser und Kleine Redoutensaal) of the Empress Maria Theresa in the Hofburg Palace, both now used to hold special events.

with the help of the Vienna fire brigade who were clearing the building that I was at last able to extract him from the admiring group and take him out to my car. Knowing that the rest of the party would be standing outside a locked door, I drove fast. Etkind settled himself comfortably, stretched out his legs for a better purchase and said affably: "One day you must come to Leningrad, you'd love to drive there—large, wide, empty streets." Since then I have dreamed, Toad-like, of tearing down the almost deserted Nevsky Prospect, but in the meantime Etkind, about whom Auden worried greatly as time went on, mainly on account of his friendship with Sacharow,[76] has left Russia and is living and working in France. And so there they all were, a not too friendly row of faces gazing over the bannisters on the second floor as we puffed our way upstairs: Auden, Kallman, Mary MacCarthy, the Toynbees,[77] the author and critic Hilde Spiel[78] and a Danish journalist friend. But over drink and food the party soon cheered up, and Mary sighed: "What heaven it is to get away from that man Reich-Ranicki!" There was a chorus of assent.

In August 1966 *The Bassarids* had had its première at the Salzburg Festival. It is an Opera Seria with Intermezzo in One Act based on *The Bacchae* of Euripides by Auden and Kallman. The following year, Auden was invited to deliver the opening address—a highly festive occasion, and his speech would be widely reported. By late April he had already made a draft,

---

76 Andrei Sakharov (1921–1989), Soviet physicist, human rights activist, and Nobel Prize laureate; subject to internal exile in the USSR 1980–1986.

77 Arnold Toynbee (1888–1975), leading English historian and specialist of international affairs, former director of studies at Chatham House and professor at the London School of Economics, and his second wife, Veronica Boulter Toynbee (1894–1980)

78 Hilde Spiel (1911–1990), aka Grace Hanshaw and Jean Lenoir, Austrian writer, journalist, and former general secretary of the Austrian PEN Center.

and he asked me for my comments. He had, he said, built in
a good deal of criticism, but could he get away with it? Was the
package sufficiently decorative? After a quick read through
I looked up and caught Auden's enquiring eye. What on earth
could I say? No amount of packaging could disguise the fact
that this was a full frontal attack on the policy behind the
Salzburg Festival and its administration; it appeared to be
wholly negative and the estimated length of half an hour was
probably too long. Towards the end, where he should be rid-
ing high in an appeal for devotion to optimal standards in
music and the arts in general and opera in particular, he was
grumbling about the erratic workings of the curtain in the
Festspielhaus and the lack of canteen facilities for the scene-
shifters. It was a horrible anticlimax. How could one tell him
this in such a way as to get results without offending him?
And there was another thing: he should be advised to rehearse.
Auden understood all the nuances of the German language,
but his spoken German was not as good as he seemed to think,
and his delivery was apt to become almost incomprehensible.

The New York postmark usually meant an announcement
of domestic disaster and a request for help, and the winter
of 1967 brought serious disruption to the peaceful running
of the house at Kirchstetten. Auden's poem to Emma Eiermann begins in German:

Liebe Frau Emma,
na, was hast du denn gemacht?

and it contains just about all there is to say about her, and
her relationship with Auden and Kallman.[79] How, the poet

---

79 "Elegy" (in memoriam Emma Eiermann ob. November 4, 1967) in
    the collection *City without Walls* (1969).

exclaims, could she go and die when they were both away—and what about the cats—they had to be destroyed. But when his letter to me arrived he didn't yet know that: it contains an urgent plea to hurry over to Kirchstetten and find out what on earth was happening to the animals. He couldn't bear to think—it was late November—that they were prowling around, unfed and shut out of her cottage. Later on he seemed to be rather upset that no one came forward to adopt one or two of the cats; the others were strays.

In February 1968 he flew over to Vienna to interview Frau Strobl after the death of Emma Eiermann. We were lunching together at the Opern-Café and this was one of the very few occasions when I kept a note of what had been said. Auden had frequently taken a stand against drug-taking, and had made his attitude clear in a number of lectures and interviews. In October 1967, for instance, he brought up the subject in a lecture at Eliot College, and now I told him I was glad he had been saying to young people in England that LSD is a dead duck for creative workers. This led to a long account of the experiments with LSD and mescalin that he himself had carried out in the company of his doctor. He was perfectly certain that no original line of poetry and no work of art had ever been created under the influence of drugs, and he was convinced that Aldous Huxley did a lot of harm by publishing his experiences with mescalin, and making people believe it to be an artistic experience. The point is, he said, that young people need to discover who and what they are. And LSD doesn't tell them, it is a purely passive effect in which there is alienation from self. You concentrate on things—a chair, the ceiling etc.,—and people become unimportant. There is a curious effect in listening to music: it is intolerable as the sounds lose their interrelation and form. Basically, what you achieve is a mild degree of schizophrenia.

After the experiment was over, he and the doctor went round to the local pub. Suddenly, through a window he saw a postman waving at him, and thought my God, this is it. Later on, the postman said "I waved at you, why didn't you answer?" An interview he gave to the *Sunday Telegraph*, published on October 29, 1967, under the headline "On drugs and drivel" adds to what he said in the Opern-Café. Much of it is vintage Auden: "Mandrake met W.H. Auden last week to a background of, not redbrick, but dazzling, chalk-white college buildings, with miniskirted freshers looking overwhelmed at having Auden pacing all their fresh-laid corridors in his carpet slippers and Sloppy Joe T-shirt marked with the Hobbit motif of the Tolkien fan club. "Now, I live a lot of the time in New York. You can live really quietly there, you know," says Auden, and anyway Britain he finds on every trip getting increasingly Americanised "and vulgar and still more vulgar. It must be the first time in history that culture has spread from the bottom up. The Establishment latches on last of all to what the mass does first. And London is so provincial. Paris is provincial. Berlin is provincial. But New York—it's dirty and a damned dangerous place to live in sometimes, but at least it isn't provincial.".... About drug-taking activities in some British universities, Auden says firmly he is an anti-drug man, "although I *have* taken them myself by way of experiment. By saying that, I don't want Mr. Quintin Hogg[80] down on my neck for corrupting the young or anything ... so what I want to make absolutely clear are the three points which should help put young people right off the idea of taking drugs at all. "First, LSD is a dangerous thing—it should be taken only under medical supervision, with somebody

---

80 Quintin Hogg (1907–2001), British barrister and Conservative party members, Lord Chancellor of Great Britain 1970–74 and 1979–87.

there, because you may get the willies and end up in a loony bin. Second, if people think they're going to get any fulfilment in Art through taking drugs then they're in for a hell of a disappointment. Because on tape recordings of people under LSD it's been shown they speak absolute drivel. Thirdly, and lastly, taking drugs as a short cut to God is absolute drivel as well." It is true, that the progressive "vulgarisation" of London struck him like a blow in the face every time he went there. He seldom failed to mention the subject when he came back to Kirchstetten, and was particularly angry about the advertisements on the London Underground, which he said beat anything to be found anywhere.

* * *

Auden liked to be amused. As I mentioned earlier, he was interested, as a human phenomenon, in my mother-in-law who until she was forced to abandon it was certainly one of the worst and most dangerous drivers who ever drove the roads of Austria. She never went very fast but she had no idea where the car began and ended nor by what means it was propelled, and she drove her car as though it were a tank, ignoring all that lay in her path. I have seen her move off, the engine howling, in a series of leaps; she had clearly forgotten to release the hand-brake. Her accidents were frequent, and often bizarre, and for all this her basic attitude to traffic was usually to blame. This attitude she made clear once and for all when sitting beside the driver—my brother-in-law—on the road to St. Pölten, which was her, and for that matter Auden's, shopping town. They came to a T crossing. It is a blind corner, one is about to turn on to a main arterial road down which the traffic thunders. The law and common sense require one to stop dead, look both ways, and only then to swing across into a gap in the stream of traffic. The driver did precisely this, whereupon my mother-in-law favoured him with a withering glance and said, unforgivably: "COWARD!" This was Auden's favourite story. She caught him once when he had nipped round to the garage in Fridau to look at the state of her Volkswagen after one of the usual smashes. It may have been the time she left the road and charged through one of those telegraph poles with two legs in the shape of an inverted Y, or another time when she failed to take a bend in the road and ended up with one wheel suspended over a vertical drop into the River Pielach far below.

At events there was a long and painful silence—Mama was famous for her silences—which Auden found it difficult to break. Whenever I saw him again for the first time after his arrival in the spring, sooner or later a look of gleeful expectancy would usher in the question: "Now: tell me about ma-in-law's latest car smash." The reason why Auden himself failed one day to take a corner in Kirchstetten village and crashed I never had the courage to ask. It happened on the first day of his arrival in about April 9, 1968. A message reached me in Vienna: he had had an accident, was in St. Pölten hospital, and could I come at my convenience? As my informant thought that Auden was about to be sent home it seemed advisable to telephone the hospital and find out where he would be by the afternoon. The following conversation ensued:

"May I ask whether Professor Auden is still in hospital, presumably in the casualty department, or whether he has been sent home?"

"Professor who?"

"Auden. A – U – D – E – N, Anna Union Dora Emil Nordpol."

"The name is not familiar. I will check the records."

Pause. "No, we have no one of that name here."

"But I am informed that Professor Auden was admitted. By the way he is an American citizen."

"Ah (confidently), then I can say quite definitely that he has not been admitted here."

So I drove out to Kirchstetten. And there was Auden, a bundle of misery, sitting at the big table all by himself, his right arm and shoulder in plaster. He was a little offhand about the accident, but his memories of the hospital which he had just left by taxi were unimpaired. They hadn't exactly put out the red carpet. For a long time, the first and only attention he had received was from a man who wanted name and address and all relevant details and, above all, "how I proposed to pay for the treatment."

Soon I was asking what I could do for him and in what order. What was the most urgent thing? "I'm almost out of gin." Perhaps I would be kind enough to ring up Wild, the grocers on the Neuer Markt in Vienna, and ask them to send some down. But why, I asked, couldn't I drive to Böheimkirchen right away and fetch some? They'd have the usual brands. No, call up Wild. Back in the Neulinggasse I rang up that high-quality emporium and gave the order. "Are you," it seemed sensible to ask, "delivering in that district during the next few days?" "We virtually *never* deliver to the country, Madam, but we always make a special trip for the Herr Professor." After a shocked silence I said: "It's no business of mine, but that's a pretty pricey way of buying the same make of gin as he could get at the local grocer's." "Quite right, Madam," said the cheerful voice, "But that has been the Herr Professor's usual practice for some years. Who am I to criticise?" A carefully worded letter to the hospital was indicated. After a brief summary of events came a few lines of comment: It was not of significance, I said heavily, that Professor Auden was a poet and author of international reputation who had

been honoured by the Austrian state. A hospital was not a re-
specter of persons, and a casualty was casualty. But to dis-
claim all knowledge of a patient who was occupying a bed
in the hospital would certainly create confusion and distress
in any family which might be the victim of such a mishap.

A day or two later I went out to Kirchstetten again with
the idea of entertaining Wystan with a few horror stories
about Austrian politics or anything else that came to mind
to cheer him over the interval until Chester arrived from
Athens. He had been back to the hospital for a check-up on
the sit of the plaster, and as I walked in he grinned from ear
to ear: "What did you say to them? I was treated like royal-
ty." For the record, the hospital did in fact write a handsome
apology in reply to my letter.

Auden would often lend his car to someone or other during the winter, and one day when he and Chester turned
up to lunch at Fridau I was shown, with some amusement,
a bullet hole in the car—just below the windscreen, in line
with the driver's seat. Having had a little experience of some
of Chester's friends in Vienna I wasn't altogether surprised,
but it later transpired that I was wrong. Naturally, no one
had told me of the existence of Auden's callboy Hugie, and it
was he who, having been lent the car, was involved in events
which led to his arrest and imprisonment. In the end, the
car became a total wreck, and the circumstances are the subject of various increasingly frantic letters from Auden before and after Christmas 1968. In December, Chester's Greek
friend Jean Boras[81] who often stayed with the two men in
Kirchstetten, was in Vienna and using the car. One day, on
the road between Vienna and Kirchstetten he collided with

---

81 Yannis Boras (1942–1968), a young Greek soldier who became Kall-
    man's lover for five years, until his death in 1968.

a lorry head on and was killed instantly. I was away at the time and only got back to the Neulinggasse shortly before Christmas, to find a letter from Auden telling me what had happened. Chester had been so prostrated with grief that he, Auden, had hardly been able to understand him on the telephone line from Athens, but he believed that he must be in Vienna. Would I look for him and see what I could do? The thought of Chester's state of mind, alone in Vienna over Christmas, was blood-chilling, and my imagination ran away with me. A protracted search produced no signs that he had been in Austria at all, and it finally turned out that he had never left Athens. Letters flew to and fro on the subjects of: release of corpse, release of wrecked car and/or papers, with Auden becoming increasingly impatient ("I am in despair") over the inaction both of officialdom and of his lawyers. He was learning the hard way that to attempt to carry out any form of business in Vienna between the last days before Christmas and the Feast of the Epiphany on January 6th is a sheer waste of time; during the Twelve Days of Christmas not even a partridge in a pear tree moves. When Auden and Kallman got back to Austria in April Chester was still profoundly shaken up and I remember Auden's anxiety, saying to me, "I don't know how he's going to get through the summer." And it struck me: what a contrast between these two writers: the lesser poet but much younger man, cooking too much rich food for the entirely sedentary life that they both led, but otherwise with little purpose left. And the far greater and much older poet, with his regular hours of work and his considerable output. The days of their very fruitful collaboration on opera libretti were already over; what remained was the *Times* crossword.

It was so easy, I think, to make fun of the slightly old-maidish ways of the house. In all those amusing and essen-

tially true articles in newspapers and glossy magazines the
tendency is to leave out this all-important fact: Auden was
a very hard-working, systematic, self-disciplined writer, who
knew, none better, how nice it is to sit sipping a cool drink
in the shade of a tree, whiling away the hours, looking with
contentment upon his flowers and his asparagus beds. This
he did, but having worked steadily through from 9 o'clock
until lunchtime. And much of the bosky contentment, the
cool drinks and so on, were simply owing to the presence of
guests, including the journalist with his sharp eye. So that
these sometimes rather rib- nudging descriptions of this un-
conventional household leave it altogether to us to remember that in the last dozen years of his life, Auden was writing several volumes of poetry, opera libretti, translating the
Elder Edda, the *Italian Journey*, Dag Hammarskjöld's *Markings*,[82]
and other works, editing *The Dyer's Hand*,[83] the *Faber Book of
Aphorisms*,[84] his *Commonplace Book*,[85] *Forewords and Afterwords*,
and that heavenly compilation the *Nineteenth Century Book of
Minor Poets*.[86] He was reading over an enormous field, writing
and delivering lectures, writing articles and book reviews—

---

82 *Vägmärken*, the posthumous publication of the former UN Secretaty-
General's private journal. The English translation was done by the
Swedish translator Leif Sjöberg and corrected by Auden who also
wrote a foreword.
83 *The Dyer's Hand and Other Essays*, a collection of essays and articles published by Auden in 1962.
84 *The Faber (Viking) Book of Aphorisms: A Personal Selection*, an anthology
of 3,000 aphorisms from various writers, thinkers, and savants, selected and edited by Auden and Louis Kronenberger, published in
1962.
85 *A Certain World: A Commonplace Book*, an anthology of passages and
quotations from other authors selected by Auden and published in
1970.
86 *Nineteenth-Century British Minor Poets*, an anthology of minor poets
born between 1770 and 1870, selected and edited by Auden and published in 1966.

sometimes they were demanding publications such as Emily Anderson's[87] three volume *Letters of Beethoven*—which he gave me, the blank pages are filled with his notes—and even a new twelve volume annotated translation of the Bible. In any case, the sacred beast in his lair was probably much wittier than most strangers who came to view the set-up.

On 19th May 1970 I was mildly horrified (I write in German but do not translate into it) to get a telegram asking, "If I sent half hour speech in a few days could you translate soon into German – Love Wystan." On the principle: say yes now, worry afterwards, I agreed. He was to deliver the speech a couple of weeks later in the small country town of Neulengbach in the presence of the governor of Lower Austria. After making a draft, I sent both texts to my husband so that he could polish up my version. It had not been easy. *"Sehr verehrter Herr Landeshauptmann, meine Damen und Herren*: I hope you will pardon me if I speak somewhat personally. I do so, not out of vanity, but because I do not wish to give the impression that I am attempting to lay down absolute laws which are valid for all. I give you my experiences as a poet, in the hope that you will be able to compare them with yours, and form your own judgement about them. Most of what I know about the writing of poetry, or at least about the kind I am interested in writing, I discovered long before I took any interest in poetry itself. Between the ages of six and twelve, I spent a great many of my waking hours in the fabrication of a private secondary sacred world, the basic elements of which were a) a limestone landscape mainly derived from the Pennine Moors in the North of England and

---

87 Emily Anderson (1891–1962), Irish scholar specialising in German and music history. Anderson spent 30 years working in the British Foreign Office and was appointed OBE in 1943 for work in the Middle East.

b) an industry—lead-mining. It is no doubt psychologically significant that my sacred world was autistic—that is to say, I had no wish to share it with others nor could I have done so. However, though constructed for and inhabited by myself alone, I needed the help of others, my parents in particular, in collecting its basic materials; others had to procure for me the necessary text-books on geology and machinery, maps, catalogues, guide-books and photographs, and, when occasion offered, to take me down real mines, tasks which they performed with unfailing patience and generosity.

From this activity, I learned certain principles which I was later to find applied to all artistic fabrication. First, whatever other elements it may include, the initial impulse to create a secondary world is a feeling of awe aroused by encounters, in the Primary World, with sacred beings or events. This feeling of awe is an imperative, that is to say, one is not free to choose the object or the event that arouses it. Though every work of art is a secondary world, it cannot be constructed ex nihilo, but is a selection from and a recombination of the contents of the Primary World. Even the 'purest' poem, in the French Symboliste sense, is made of words which are not the poet's private property, but the communal creation of the linguistic group to whom he belongs, so that their meaning can be looked up in a dictionary. Secondly, in constructing my private world, I discovered that, though this was a game, or rather precisely because it was a game—that is to say, not a necessity like eating or sleeping, but something I was free to do or not as a chose—it could not be played without rules. Absolute freedom is meaningless: freedom can only be realised in a choice between alternatives. A secondary world, be it a poem, or a game of football or bridge, must be as much a world of law as the Primary, the only difference being that in the world of games one is free to decide what its laws shall be. But to all games as to real life, Goethe's lines apply.

In der Beschränkung zeigt sich erst der Meister
Und das Gesetz nur kann uns Freiheit geben.[88]

As regards my particular lead-mining world, I decided, or rather, without conscious decision I instinctively felt, that I must impose two restrictions upon my freedom of fantasy. In choosing what objects were to be included, I was free to select this and reject that, on condition that both were real objects in the Primary World, to choose, for example, between two kinds of water-turbine, which could be found in a text-book on mining machinery or a manufacturer's catalogue: but I was not free to invent one. In deciding how my world was to function, I could choose between two practical possibilities—a mine can be drained either by an adit or a pump—but physical impossibilities and magic means were forbidden. When I say forbidden, I mean that I felt, in some obscure way, that they were morally forbidden.

Then there came a day when the moral issue became quite conscious. As I was planning my Platonic Idea of a concentrating-mill, I ran into difficulties. I had to choose between two types of a certain machine for separating the slimes, called a buddle. One type I found more sacred or 'beautiful,' but the other type was, I knew from my reading, the more efficient. At this point I realised that it was my moral duty to sacrifice my aesthetic preference to reality or truth. When, later, I began to write poetry, I found that, for me at least,

---

88 From Goethe's sonnet "Natur und Kunst" (Nature and art) written in 1800.
    "Only self-mastered may man master be,
    And only the law can make us free."

the same obligation was binding. That is to say, I cannot accept the doctrine that, in poetry, there is a 'suspension of belief.' A poet must never make a statement simply because it sounds poetically exciting: he must also believe it to be true. This does not mean, of course, that one can only appreciate a poet whose beliefs happen to coincide with one's own. It does mean, however, that one must be convinced that the poet really believes what he says, however odd the belief may seem to oneself. Between constructing a private fantasy world for oneself alone and writing poetry, there is, of course, a profound difference. A fantasy world exists only in the head of its creator: a poem is a public verbal object intended to be read and enjoyed by others. To become conscious of others is to become conscious of historical time in various ways. The contents of a poem are necessarily past experiences, and the goal of a poem is necessarily in the future, since it cannot be read until it has been written. Again, to write a poem is to engage in an activity which human beings have practised for centuries.

If one asks why human beings make poems or paint pictures or compose music, I can see two possible answers. Firstly all the artistic media are forms of an activity peculiar to human beings, namely, Personal Speech. Many animals have impersonal codes of communications, visual, olfactory, auditory signals, by which they convey to other members of their species vital information about food, territory, sex, the presence of enemies, etc., and in social animals like the bee, such a code may be exceedingly complex. We, too, of course, often use words in the same way, as when I ask a stranger the way to the railroad station. But when we truly speak, we do something quite different. We speak as person to person in order to disclose ourselves to others and share our experiences with them, not because we must, but because we enjoy doing so. This activity is sometimes quite erroneously called 'self-expression.' If I write a poem about experiences I have had, I do so because I think it should be of interest and value to others: the fact that it has till now only been my experience is accidental. What the poet or any artist has to convey is a perception of a reality common to all, but seen from a unique perspective, which it is his duty as well as his pleasure to share with others. To small truths as well as great, St. Augustine's words apply.

> *The truth is neither mine nor his nor another's; but belongs to us all whom Thou callest to partake of it: warning us terribly, not to account it private to ourselves, lest we be deprived or it.*[89]

Then the second impulse to artistic fabrication is the desire to transcend our mortality, by making objects which, unlike ourselves, are not subject to natural death, but can remain permanently 'on hand' in the world, long after we and our society have perished. Every genuine work of art, I believe, exhibits two qualities, Nowness and Permanence.

By Nowness I mean the quality which enables an art-historian to date a work, at least, approximately. If, for example, one listens to a composition by Palestrina[90] and one by Mozart, one knows immediately that, quite aside from their artistic merits, Palestrina must have lived earlier than Mozart: he could not possibly have written as he did after Mozart. By Permanence, I mean that the work continues to have relevance and importance long after its creator is dead. In the history of Art, unlike the history of Science, no genuine

---

89 From Augustine's *Confessions*, Book XII, Chapter 25.
90 Giovanni Pierluigi da Palestrina (c.1525–1594), Italian composer of the late Renaissance period and leading member of the Roman School of composers.

work of art is made obsolete by a later work. Past science is of interest only to the historian of science, not to what scientists are doing at this moment. Past works of art, on the other hand, are of the utmost importance to the contemporary practitioner. Every artist tries to produce something now, but in the hope that, in time, it will take its proper place in the tradition of his art. And he cannot produce anything significantly original unless he knows well what has already been done; that is to say, he cannot 'rebel' against the past without having a profound reverence for it. There are periods in history when the arts develop uninterruptedly, each generation building on the achievements of the previous generation. There are other periods when radical breaks seem to be necessary. However, when they are, one will generally find that the 'radical' artist does not disown the past, but finds in works of a much earlier period or in those of a culture (other) than his own, the clue as to what he should do now.

In my own case, for example, I know how much I owe to Anglo-Saxon and Medieval Poetry. When I review the contemporary artistic scene, it strikes me how extraordinarily fortunate men like Stravinsky, Picasso, Eliot, etc., that is, those persons we think of as the founders of 'modern' art, were in being born when they were, so that they came to manhood before 1914. Until the First World War, western society was still pretty much what it had been in the nineteenth century. This meant that for these artists, the felt need to create something new arose from an artistic imperative, not a historic imperative. No one asked himself: 'What is the proper kind of music to compose or picture to paint or poem to write in the year 1912?' Secondly, their contemporary audiences were mostly conservative, but honestly so. Those, for instance, who were scandalised by Le Sacre du Printemps, may seem to us now to have been old fogies, but their reaction was genuine. They did not say to themselves: 'Times have changed and we must change with them in order not to be left behind.' Here are a few statements by Stravinsky to which the young, whether artists or critics would do well to listen and ponder over.

> In my youth the new music grew out of, and in reaction to, traditions, whereas it appears to be evolving to-day as much from social needs as interior artistic ones... The status of new music as a category is another incomparable. It had none at all in my early years, being in fact categorically opposed, and often with real hostility, But the unsuccess of composers of my generation at least kept them from trading on success, and our unsuccess may have been less insidious than the automatic superlatives which nowadays kill the new by absorbing it to death.

> The use of the new hardware naturally appears to the new musician as 'historically imperative'; but music is made out of musical imperatives, and the awareness of historical processes is probably best left to future and different kinds of wage-earners.

* * *

In times, like our own, of rapid social change and political crisis, there is always a danger of confusing the principles governing political action and those governing artistic fabrication. The most important of such confusions are three. Firstly, one may come to think of artistic fabrication as a form of political action. Every citizen, poets included, has a duty to be politically 'engagé,' that is, to play a responsible part in seeing that the society of which he is a member shall function properly and improve. But the poet, *qua* poet, has only one political function. Since language is his medi-

um, it is his duty, by his own example, to defend his mother-
tongue against corruption by demagogues, journalists, the
mass-media, etc. As Karl Kraus[91] said: *Die Sprache ist die Mutter, nicht das* [sic] *Magd, des Gedankens*,[92] and when language
loses its meaning, its place is taken by violence. Of course,
the poet may use political and social events as subject-matter for poems—they are as much a part of human experience as love or nature—but he must never imagine that his
poems have the power to affect the course of history. The
political and social history of Europe would be what it has
been if Dante, Shakespeare, Goethe, Michael Angelo, Titian, Mozart, Beethoven, etc. had never existed. Where political and social evils are concerned, only two things are effective: political action and straightforward, truthful, detailed
journalistic rapportage of the facts. The Arts are powerless.
The second confusion, of which Plato is the most famous example, is to take artistic fabrication as the model for a good
society. Such a model, if put into practice, is bound to produce a tyranny. The aim of the artist is to produce an object
which is complete and will endure without change. In the
'city' of a poem, there are always the same inhabitants doing exactly the same jobs forever. A society which was really like a good poem, embodying the aesthetic virtues of order, economy and subordination of the detail to the whole,
would be a nightmare of horror for, given the historical reality of actual men, such a society could only come into being through selective breeding, extermination of the physically and mentally unfit, absolute obedience to its Director,

---

91 Karl Kraus (1874–1936), Austrian writer, journalist, essayist, play-
    wright, and satirist, founder of the satirical journal *Die Fackel* (The
    torch).
92 "Language is the mother, not the handmaid, of thought" from "Aph-
    orismen," in *Die Fackel,* no. 288, October 11, 1909, 10.

a large slave class kept out of sight in cellars, and the strict-est censorship of the Arts, forbidding anything to be said which is out of keeping with the official 'line.' The third con-fusion, typical of our western 'free' societies at this time, is the opposite of Plato's, namely to take political action as the model for artistic fabrication. Political action is a necessity, that is to say, at (e)very moment something has to be done, and it is momentary—action at this moment is immediate-ly followed by another action at the next. Artistic fabrica-tion, on the other hand, is voluntary—the alternative to one work of art can be no work of art—and the artistic object is permanent, that is to say, immune to historical change. The attempt to model artistic fabrication on political action can therefore, only reduce it to momentary and arbitrary 'hap-penings,' a conformism with the tyranny of the immediate moment which is far more enslaving and destructive of in-tegrity than any conformism with past tradition.

At this point, a little digression on the subject of 'free' verse, which seems now to be almost universal among young poets. Though excellent examples, the poems of D.H. Law-rence, for example, exist, they are, in my opinion, the excep-tion, not the rule. The great virtue of formal metrical rules is that they forbid automatic responses and, by forcing the poet to have second thoughts, free him from the fetters of self. All too often, the result of not having a fixed form to be true to is a self-indulgence which in the detached reader can only cause boredom. Further, in my experience, contrary to what one might expect, the free-verse poets sound much more like each other than those who write in fixed forms. Whatever freedom may do, it does not, it would seem, make for originality. What, then, can the Arts do for us? In my opinion, they can do two things. They can, as Dr. Johnson said, 'enable us a little better to enjoy life or a little better to endure it.'[93] And, because they are objects permanently on hand in the world, they are the chief means by which the living are able to break bread with the dead, and, without a communication with the dead, I do not believe that a fully human civilised life is possible. Perhaps, too, in our age, the mere making of a work of art is itself a political act. So long as artists exist, making what they please or think they ought to make, even if their works are not terribly good, they remind the Management of something managers need to be reminded of, namely, that the managed are people with faces, not anonymous numbers, that *Homo Laborans* is also *Homo Ludens*. And now, I hope those of you who know no English will forgive me if I conclude these remarks with a light poem of my own, entitled 'Doggerel by a Senior Citizen.'"

To what extent parts of this lecture had been said or written before is immaterial, it is still surprising that Auden chose to repeat it in Neulengbach. If here and there he

Adopted what I would disown
The preacher's loose immodest tone

in the main, such a closely argued statement must surely have floated past the ear of most of his listeners. This would not, I think, have been because of an innate lack of intelligence on their part, but because the Austrian and the German academic mind tends towards compartmentalised thought more than is the case among well-educated Americans, British, and French people who may have acquired the ability to survey one discipline in terms of another.

---

93 The actual line is: "The only end of writing is to enable the readers better to enjoy life, or better to endure it" from *A Free Enquiry* (1757).

This exceedingly demanding speech tells one something else about Auden: he never talked down to people. They would absorb as much as they were able to, as much as they were ready for; and someone would have understood a great deal. Auden's attitude towards language as a means towards 'artistic fabrication' is I think in the exact sense of the word sacramental. Holding the insights that he did into the nature of the poet's struggle with the primary world, it is hardly surprising that he should have held strong views on modern translations of the Bible—a subject he often came back to in conversation—and revised liturgies. The new banality offended his acute sense of the power contained in words and phrases which have brought mankind into mystical contact with the primary world: Darkness, Silence, Nothing, Death, and all those things which are held sacred by any particular cultural group. It is consistent that Auden was suspicious of Eng. Lit. textual analysis; that he felt the importance that— gross misunderstanding apart—the reader should receive something from a poem; it is consistent that he should have laughed when he told me that some earnest person wanted to know just what he had meant by a word written thirty years ago. 'Ridiculous! How should I know?' It always seemed that as the years passed Auden became more and more English; this natural process of reverting to type annoyed Chester who would expostulate at signs of it. He liked to listen to the cool, rounded tones of the British county gentry, he intensely admired *Akenfield*, he loved the Lucia novels by E.F. Benson, he happily read and reviewed *The History of the British Nannie*,[94] and he was addicted to English detective novels— his collection is now at Fridau.

---

94 A reference to Jonathan Gathorne-Hardy's *The Rise and Fall of the British Nanny* (1972), for which Auden wrote a review for *The Observer*.

I dropped in one early afternoon on my way to Vienna, just to leave something for him, I forgot what. Auden came pounding down the rickety outside staircase, greeted me with his usual warmth, urged me to come in, to stay ... No no, I said, we're both busy, I must get on. "Oh!" he exclaimed, and it was as though he were begging me not to infringe the most basic rule of British hospitality: "But you *can't* go without having a cup of tea!" That study of his is so bare now: it is "The Cave of Making"[95] which he wished he could have shown to Louis MacNeice,[96] and the house and garden.

> ... Devoid of
> flowers and family photographs, all is subordinate
> here to a function, designed to
> discourage daydreams—hence windows averted from plausible
> videnda but admitting a light one
> could mend a watch by—and to sharpen hearing: reached
> by an outside staircase, domestic
> noises and odours, the vast background of natural
> life are shut off. Here silence
> is turned into objects.

To write to Auden unnecessarily would have been to encroach on his time. But Chester spent the whole of one winter in Vienna and I could hardly resist describing a party in Chester's flat. Afterwards, I had given a lift home to a carload of people including one whose pockets, had I but known it, were stuffed with Chester's money—lifted from a jacket hanging on the bedroom door. The party itself had been all

---

95 The poem "Cave of Making" was dedicated to Louis MacNiece and published in the collection *About the House* (1963).
96 Frederick Louis MacNeice (1907–1963), Irish poet and playwright, and member of the Auden Group.

but wrecked by a loudly argumentative individual who succeeded in clearing the sitting room altogether as the guests
gradually slunk off to the kitchen, refugees from his abra-
sive but tedious presence. Auden's reply was: "So! You encountered the one-whose-name-we-never-mention. Why Chester
should have been so foolish as to invite him to a party I cannot imagine. If he is to be seen at all he is to be seen alone."
My next sighting of this cloven-hooved adjunct to the Viennese literary scene was at Auden's funeral, where I watched
him work his way up the procession to the church until he
found the place he sought: immediately behind the coffin
among the chief mourners. Wondering at this, and remem-
bering Wystan's sinister euphemism, I subsequently asked
Chester whether Auden had ever liked the man. "LIKED
him?" shrieked Chester. "Why, he crossed himself whenever his name was mentioned." In that same letter to New York
I mentioned that a friend of his had quoted him as using
the term—as a definition of humour—"serious insistence
on unseriousness." His response was as follows: "X has a genius for subtle misrepresentation. 'Serious insistence on unseriousness' telescopes two distinct convictions of mine, falsifying both.

One. I believe it to be a serious moral error when an artist overestimates the importance of art and, by implication,
of himself. One must admit that the political history of Europe, with the same horrors, would be what it has been, if
Dante, Shakespeare, Goethe, Titian, Mozart, et al, had never existed. Two. I believe that the only way in which, to-day
at any rate, one can speak seriously about serious matters
(the alternative is silence) is comically. I have enormously
admired—and been influenced by—the tradition of Jewish
humor. More than any other people, surely, they have seen
in serious matters, that is to say, human suffering, the con-

tradictions of human existence, and the relation between
man and God, occasions for humorous expression. e.g. 'If
the rich could hire other people to die for them, the poor
could make a wonderful living,' or, 'Truth rests with God
alone, and little bit with me,' or 'God will provide—ah, if only he would till He does so.'" After a brief domestic chroni-
cle he adds that a friend of his who teaches schizophrenics
had a seventeen year old girl who was interested in poetry.
Asked what poets she liked, she mentioned Auden. "I happen
to know him quite well," said the friend. To which the girl
in astonishment: "You mean to say, he's still alive?" (Auden
was about 58 at the time).

That deeply scored face which struck awe into so many
people who saw him, that battlefield so mercilessly displayed
above dozens upon dozens of newspaper articles: when I look
at my own photographs of him I am appalled at the speed of
the development. It was a head straight out of the Icelandic
sagas, or a prehistoric head from the bogs of Jutland. Auden
should have been carved, much larger than life, by Henry
Moore[97] and placed in effigy on a high hill. Abruptly, the
way most statements emerged from Auden, he said one day
at lunch: "Kokoschka wants to paint me." It appears that Oskar Kokoschka[98] had written and asked him to come to Swit-
zerland. But Auden felt it was too much of an effort, and evidently the much older man felt the same way, so that nothing
came of it. It is a great pity, because for one thing they would
have enjoyed each other's company, and the sight of these

---

97 Henry Moore (1898–1986), English artist best known for semi-ab-
stract monumental bronze sculptures.
98 Oskar Kokoschka (1886–1980), Austrian artist, poet, and playwright
best known for his intense expressionistic portraits and landscapes,
as well as his theories on vision which influenced the Viennese Ex-
pressionist movement.

physically so oddly similar men sitting together must have fired some onlooker if only to the extent of taking a historic snapshot. Nor does Auden's closing remark on the subject provide much compensation for the lack of the portrait, though the thought satisfied him. "After all," he said, as he reached for his wine glass and narrowed his eyes to slits against the sunlight seeping in from the garden, "After all, I AM a Kokoschka painting." But the causes: the question needs to be answered. Why was Auden, in his sixties and indeed much earlier, a prematurely aged man? *"Ein alter Mann,"* one or two German obituarists were to write, but without surprise, or: "the aged poet"—when he was 68! Surely not. There is one explanation which I place on record only after much hesitation. Sometime after Auden's death, Chester Kallman gave me his explanation for the evidence that Wystan had become older than his years warranted: he put the phenomenon down to Benzedrine. "For how long?" Oh, said Chester, he began right back in his early years in the States. And he had carried on right rough, only dropping the habit when he came to spend his summers in Austria. Most people now have forgotten about Benzedrene; other things have taken its place. Chester reminded me that it was the stimulant with the help of which airmen in wartime, examinees, doctors, and so on, could keep themselves going in a state of complete wakefulness to carry them through a period of temporary stress. Taken for a restricted purpose, perhaps by a surgeon faced with operations round the clock after a major disaster, it was a blessing. Physical reserves would be replaced later when the emergency was over. But to take Benzedrine over a long period meant—I am quoting Kallman and subject to correction—using up one's body at an accelerated rate with the obvious consequence that it would become prematurely aged. It would be difficult to think of any reason why Chester should say this if it were not substantially true. As to why Auden should have felt he needed such a powerful stimulant, over and above those which modern man indulges in as a matter of course -coffee, tea, alcohol and cigarettes—his friends of those years can answer.

Perhaps an extract from Edmund Wilson's "W.H. Auden in America"[99] is helpful: it is one of a collection of critical essays edited by Monroe Spears[100] and published in 1964: the operative phrase lies buried in the quotation. "Since becoming an American citizen, the poet has not ceased to explore, to roam—he has covered more ground in this country than most Americans do, and he now spends every summer in Italy. This spring he returns to England to be lecturer on poetry at Oxford. It is a part of his role to go everywhere, be accessible to all sorts of people, serve interestedly and conscientiously in innumerable varied capacities: on the staff of a Middle Western college; at a cultural congress in India; on a grand jury in New York City, deciding the fate of gangsters; on a committee of the American Academy, making handouts to needy writers. He has above all withstood the ordeal of America through a habitation of seventeen years; he has even 'succeeded' here. And he has made all these exploits contribute to the work of a great English poet who is also—in the not mundane sense—one of the great English men of the world."

During the uprising in Czechoslovakia in the early autumn of 1968 Vienna was filled with people who had come across the border bent on emigration, or simply to snuff the air outside their own country and explore the possibil-

---

99 First published in the British political and cultural journal *New Statesman and Nation*, June 9, 1956.
100 Monroe Spears (1916–1998), American professor and literary critic, and both author and editor of several books on American and British poetry.

ities. Many people had strangers in their houses and Auden wanted to do his bit. As he was just leaving Kirchstetten he left it to me to choose a suitable family, and having done so I wrote to him c/o Heyworth, 32 Bryanston Square, London W.1. A reply is dated 15 October 1968:

"Got back from Oxford yesterday and found your letter waiting.

1) I think I ought to take the couple in, but I must leave it to you to decide whether they are O.K. If they are, all rooms, including my study (which can't be heated) are open to them.

2) How much money will they need to keep going? And how shall I make the arrangements for payment?

3) Will they be able to find work or emigrate before I return in April, when I'm afraid there will not be room for them?

4) I'm worried about how they will get gas cylinders for cooking from Neulengbach, since, presumably, they have no car. I expect someone in the village will help. If and when they come, I must know in advance so that I can write a note to the Burgomeister..."

The couple found somewhere else to live in a less remote place, the emergency was soon over and Auden did not disguise his relief:

"77 St. Mark's Place, N.Y.C. Nov. 6th.

Many thanks for your letter. Of course, selfishly, I'm rather relieved. How horrid one is! The U.S. is grim."

Auden was an extraordinarily generous person. An evening at the Opern-Café comes to mind. Wystan and Chester had been to a performance over the road and had asked me to join them afterwards. It was hoped that Balanchine[101] would join us, but to my disappointment he never turned up. Conversation was lively, and the more so, the greater the contrast with the enforced silence of a young Austrian whose identity was never fully revealed, though Chester muttered to me: "Wystan is helping with his studies at the College of Technology." When the party broke up it turned out that the young man lived in my direction, so I took him home, and in my car he opened his mouth and spoke, and what he said became engraved on my mind. "Who is Professor Auden?" he asked. "Tell me about him. Is he an important man?" This is the cue for a story which, though with names omitted, should be placed on record. It must have been in about 1949 or 1950 that an American woman was travelling by train in Austria. In the carriage were two Austrian boys in their early teens. The three got into conversation; the woman asked a number of questions and heard the boys' story. Their father was an artist, they lived in a village on a lakeside and went to the local high school. Yes, they would be leaving school at fifteen, one of them would go as an apprentice to the local printer's. No, there was no money for further education, there was no grammar school nearby, the family couldn't afford boarding school fees, nor lodgings. Not long after this chance encounter the family heard that Auden would like to pay for the boys' education. They went through grammar school in Innsbruck and never looked back; both made swift careers in industry. I have the impression that Auden did meet the family in later years; nothing was ever further from my mind than to bring up the story

---

101 George Balanchine (1904–1983), Georgian-American ballet choreographer, founder of the New York City Ballet and its director for 35 years.

with Auden. It was disinterested generosity of a rare order. In the light of this kindness to Austrian citizens, it is sad, and ironical too, that his final years in Austria should have brought him into conflict with the tax authorities. He had felt at peace in Kirchstetten:

Here, though, I feel as at home
as you did: the same
short-lived creatures re-utter
the same care-free songs,
orchards cling to the regime
they know, from April's
rapid augment of colour
till boisterous Fall,
when at each stammering gust
apples thump the ground.[102]

And in his "Prologue at Sixty":

Though the absence of hedge-rows is odd to me
(no Whig landlord, the landscape vaunts,
ever empired on Austrian ground),
this unenglish tract after ten years
into my love has looked itself...

But then worry invaded it. While all the time believing himself not to be liable for income tax, debts to the fiscus were in fact running up to such an extent that a mortgage was placed on the property in Kirchstetten. The final amount was A.S. 930,000. What this meant to Auden was that instead of being able to take things a bit more easily, he had to pay

---

102 From the poem "Joseph Weinheber."

out pretty well all that he had put on one side, and return to the lecture circuit in the States, a prospect which he viewed with dread. "Do you know," he said to me, "they're accusing me of having been inspired by the Austrian landscape! The Weinheber poem and all that." I said: "You wrote the poem in Berlin" and he shrugged. At that time I had no idea how serious the whole thing was. As the result of an appeal in high quarters the sum was reduced by about half, and was fully paid up. At some point, the document is undated, Auden composed a statement, consisting of three pages of typescript, giving his point of view in this extraordinary affair. One day, if the whole official correspondence is published, this document with the rest will be numbered among the curiosities of literary history. Having disposed of the "accusations" that he had a "material interest" in Austria, that he had been awarded the state prize for literature, and that a road in Kirchstetten had been named after him (he requested the local authorities, by the way, not to do so until after his death, but they disregarded his wish), he continued: "You go on to say, correctly, that I have written a few poems on Austrian themes. To this I should like to make three observations: 1. I have never received so much as a penny for my poetry in Austria. A few of them were translated into German, but in this case the translators received the money, not I."

The statement is in German translation, what follows is my own re-translation back into English and not the original.

"I believe you are not aware how it is that poems are written. What is generally taken to be the subject is only a point of view, an occasion, in order to give expression to certain thoughts about nature, about God, history, mankind etc. which the poet may have had in his head for a very long time. I wrote a poem, for instance, for the 20th anniversary of the death of Josef Weinheber. But basically, the poem has to do with other things: firstly with the love which every good poet, of whatever nationality he may be, has for his mother tongue, and secondly with what has happened since the war in the countries that lost it, that is to say, not only Austria, but also Germany and Italy. Then again: in 1964 I wrote a poem with the title 'Whitsunday in Kirchstetten' because I happened to be there at the time. But the place is unimportant. What this poem is actually about is the question: 'What is the significance for a Christian of the Feast of Pentecost?' And this applies to all countries alike. I believe that you fail to understand the financial situation of a poet. A novelist can, if he is successful, earn a good deal of money with his books. A poet cannot do that, even if he is very well known, because poems are only read by a minority. Far and away the greater part of my income derives, therefore, not from the sale of my volumes of verse, but from book reviews, translations, lectures, etc., activities which have nothing to do with Austria. And while on the subject of translations: you say correctly, that I have a great interest in German and Austrian literature—I might add, also in its music, but I have no need to come to Austria to read or to hear them." Auden goes on to the length of time spent annually in Austria, and concludes: "One last word. If this in my view utterly unjustified nonsense does not cease, I shall leave Austria never to return, which both for me and perhaps too for the shopkeepers of Kirchstetten would be very sad. But one thing I cannot conceal from you, gentlemen: if this should come about, the consequence might be a scandal of world-wide dimensions."

The news reached me over the car radio on the motorway near Linz, and I headed straight for Kirchstetten on the off-chance that Chester might already have come home. Wystan had died in the night of 28/29 September, and the fact blotted out all else. Why had I gone to Linz and missed his last reading at the Society for Literature? I had talked it over with him a few days earlier, saying that I was exasperated at finding myself committed to a meeting in Linz which I yearned to cut; particularly as I should like him to make use of my flat and perhaps spend the night there. I was glum, and he cheered me up, saying that I'd heard it all before, and I must come over afterwards and he'd tell me how it had gone off. There was all too much time on the motorway to react, and I fought against what seemed to be unreasonable waves of emotion. Don't exaggerate, I told myself, don't flatter yourself that you have the right to mourn. Think of Chester. I am thinking of Chester; I hardly dare think of him. How will he live? Will he live? The car radio was still muttering quietly. As a distraction, I turned it up and the familiar voice of Friedrich Heer reviewing a book was something consoling to hold on to.

The green shutters on the door at Kirchstetten were closed, and there was no one there. I wrote a note and stuck it in the centre gap, watched by the Strobls' eternally suspicious mongrel, and drove to Fridau. An answer to the note came by telephone: Chester would like me to come over in the afternoon—by now it was Sunday. The room was full of people. On the seat behind the coffee table sat the pathetic figure whom one instinctively acknowledged as the widow. Mrs. Clark and her daughter had come up from Florence, the mayor of Kirchstetten was there, the headmistress of the high school, Frau Seitz, a writer friend of Chester's called Adolf Opel, and an assortment of unidentified young people. The expressions on the faces of the chief protagonists in what was clearly a heated discussion were not quite what one would expect at a gathering of mourners and local worthies who had come to offer their condolences. The mayor was looking stubborn, Frau

Seitz looked worried, the Clarks puzzled. Chester was hardly coherent; the rest conversed in whispers. Chester tried to explain, and gradually his wishes became clear. He hated everything in the shape of *pompes funèbres*. He wanted Wystan buried quietly and at once, if possible on Tuesday, telegrams had been sent to John Auden,[103] to Stephen Spender and others telling them to come on Tuesday morning or earlier. The mayor, Chester said, wanted a big funeral at the following weekend, with the town band out, a hearse coming to the door, representatives of the Ministry of Education, the Land and all the rest of it. He, Chester, couldn't bear it and wouldn't have it. Knowing Austrian burial customs it was evident that we were faced with a cultural clash of no mean proportions. A hurried private funeral of the kind envisaged by Chester might seem normal in western intellectual circles.

In Austria it was an affront to the decencies and carried a whiff of pauperism, suicide or both. Now the mayor had his say. "First of all," he said, "the body has not yet been released. As in all cases of sudden death in a hotel, where the circumstances are not wholly clear, there has had to be an inquest, and even with intervention, these things take time." And then: "Imagine not even informing the ministry, the department of culture of the Land government—it would be more than my job is worth." Frau Seitz now gave it as her view that Kirchstetten would hardly bury a dog in the way intended by Herr Kallman, let alone a major poet, a man moreover whom they had all known and loved. The discussion continued, the young people drifted like autumn leaves hither and thither, whispering and bearing bottles. Frau Strobl made frequent dramatic entrances for reasons which were never quite clear.

---

103 John Bicknell Auden (1903–1991), Auden's older brother, a geologist and explorer who worked for the Geological Survey of India.

It was not, it occurred to us, only a question of when and how much, but: what kind of a funeral service should it be? Auden was a practising member of the Church of England [few people would question this, but in view of two or three statements in the press that he became R.C., the fact perhaps needs emphasizing.]—or of the Episcopalian Church in the States—but he had regularly attended Mass in the Catholic Church of Kirchstetten and had wished to be buried there. Should not the Anglican chaplain in Vienna be asked to participate? No one seemed to have any ideas, but it was finally agreed that an ecumenical service would be appropriate, the texts to be spoken being left to John Auden to decide in conjunction with the clergy.

The room was stifling. It seemed that Chester needed to have fewer people around him and that the party needed to be broken up. The chance came when Chester agreed to have the funeral postponed. If my memory of events is correct, agreement was first reached only over the vital point that Tuesday was impossible and that people in England should be notified at once, leaving the final date over for the moment. This decision conveniently created a natural pause, and now the Clarks undertook to send the telegrams and were driven to the post office by Frau Strobl. We all stood up, Chester came over and asked me to carry on discussions for the funeral arrangements with the mayor and Frau Seitz. It was all, he said, more than he could bear. I must just try to hold the others in check but he would agree to anything I said. He was all right really, he was full to the brim with tranquillisers and only needed a bit of peace. We hugged each other warmly and, together with the mayor, I left in Frau Seitz's car and we drove to her house at the other end of the village. This was not the sort of talk in which one can whip through the agenda, and we took our time. If only Chester had realised it, compared with the style in which an Austrian village carries its senior citizens to the grave, what he was being asked to consent to was not a tall order.

There would be no voluntary fire brigade, no gamekeepers with their ancient ritual and their wishes for good hunting in the fields of Elysium bellowed into the open grave, no linesmen from the local railway, no representatives of the local football club, marksmen's association, et al. And since none of them would be there, they would not have to be fed afterwards. All the mayor wanted was the brass band; I felt that Wystan would have been amused, and might, if he were watching, even enjoy it, and I agreed.

Thursday was chosen to keep down the number of idle onlookers, a great concession for which I was grateful. Chester had told me that he had a phobia about hearses being brought to the door. What he wanted was for the coffin to be carried to the bottom of the hill, if not further, and only then placed in the hearse. But the thought of the weighty coffin being carried down a narrow lane, pitted with ruts and potholes and strewn with loose stones, made my hair stand on end. The mayor and Frau Seitz felt the same way, and here too, Chester later agreed to our compromise. Subsequently, I was to blame myself very much for not raising the question of who was to pay for the band. As Chester was being compelled to comply with local customs, and the district council in the person of its mayor wished to honour a citizen who had brought it great fame, it never occurred to me that it was not free of charge. Nor did it occur to Chester, whose anger at being sent in a bill precipitated a chain of events which badly hampered the efforts of the Society for Literature to preserve the house as a place of memorial for W.H. Auden. At the time, however, we thought we had troubles enough, and the misunderstanding was born.

Meanwhile the mayor was worrying about something else altogether: the safety of Auden's manuscripts and papers in the attic room. Altogether, he took a distrustful view of the fate of the house and everything in it once Chester went back to Athens. He was afraid that in his state of despair and nervous exhaustion Chester might agree to almost anything that was suggested to him with sufficient force or calculation. But to pursue this subject further would be to reach out too far beyond the death of Auden.

When I got back to the house it was to find Chester in a calmer frame of mind and body and able to talk in that gentle and affectionate way, with an occasional burst of sardonic humour, which his friends will remember, overlooking all else. In attempting a memoir of Auden in his latter years it would be unreasonable to leave Chester Kallman to play a purely walking on part, the more so as in articles by visitors to Kirchstetten Chester was invariably the fall-guy. It would be very difficult fully to understand the relationship between Auden and Kallman, and it never seemed to me that it was any business of mine to try to do so. But I saw something of Chester without Wystan: during the winter that he spent alone in Vienna in a flat in the Esslarngasse not far from my own, and when he was in hospital in St. Pölten for treatment. He was a person full of contrasts where vulgarity and second-rate humour and tastes lived side by side with a remarkable personal sensitivity and with talent and discrimination in the spheres of literature and music. It seems clear from their writings alone, that when both men went their own ways in sexual matters, Auden's heart was not involved, whereas Kallman's relationship with Jean Boras was both passionate and emotionally degrading. Both men needed each other and perhaps it would have been better if Chester had never left New York for Athens. Apart, both lapsed into squalor; together, they kept the pot boiling and the stove crackling. The daily routine was maintained, drink disciplined, and loneliness banished. When Boras died, Auden wondered how Kallman would get through the Austrian summer. When Auden died, Kallman pined away. The gathering in the livingroom on the eve of the funeral prompted that banal, well-known reflection about how much the deceased would have enjoyed it. There was the comforting presence of John Auden, Stephen Spender was there, David Luke,[104] the Clarks, Sonia Orwell.[105] There were no more conflicts of interest, no more cultural confrontations, merely a group of people bent on mutual consolation. Then Auden came home to Kirchstetten, that un-English tract. He had celebrated Kirchstetten village, the church where he sang so flat and now lies buried, and the house he lived. He had celebrated Josef Weinheber, Franz Jägerstätter,[106] Emma Eiermann and the cats. He had celebrated the whole quiet, unexciting landscape and its war-torn past and even the autobahn which lies between the church and his home, bisecting the invisible line joining one to the other. Though as we know from his statement for the taxation people, he would not want us to take him too literally. "What is taken to be the subject of a poem is only a point of view, an occasion, in order to give expression to certain thoughts about nature, about God..." In other words:

---

104 David Luke (1921–2005), British scholar of German literature, noted for his translations of Goethe, Mann, Kleist, Brothers Grimm and others.

105 Sonia Orwell (1918–1980), archivist and second wife of British writer George Orwell.

106 Franz Jägerstätter (1907–1943), Austrian conscientious objector executed by the Nazis, was later declared a martyr and beatified by the Catholic Church .

To speak is human because human to listen,
Beyond hope, for an Eighth Day,
when the creature's Image shall become the Likeness:
Giver-of-Life, translate for me
Till I accomplish my corpse at last.[107]

---

107 From "Prologue at Sixty"

In Retrospect

Since then the Auden industry has not been idle. An excellent biography was published and in this the Austrian period was dealt with but not locally researched. Edward Mendelson[108] edited Auden's early works and wrote superb commentaries. There has been a biography of Chester Kallman.[109]

Writers of PhD theses have been out here and have shaken us up, particularly Michael O'Sullivan of Trinity College, Dublin who—not speaking a word of German—organised a full-scale exhibition and an international symposium in Vienna. Peter Müller had brought Michael out to see me at Fridau in the preceding year; now he came again, and after the closure, exhausted, he spent a long weekend in the country to recover. We dug out ancient files containing original Auden manuscripts, letters, personal notes, and newspaper cuttings, and now we tried to winnow the wheat from the chaff. After some general discussion it seemed to us all that

---

108 Edward Mendelson (1946), American professor of English and Comparative literature at Columbia University.
109 This is likely a reference to Dorothy J. Farnan's 1984 account of Auden and Kallman's relationship, *Auden in Love*.

there remain certain aspects of Auden's life in Lower Austria which are not on record, or where they are, not from the worm's eye view.

As an older man he was happier here than anywhere else: he felt at home. He was at Kirchstetten not only during the summer, as is often said, but with interruptions for five months, depending on his engagements. In the course of these years he was still highly creative. So that it might, we thought, be of value to put some of those things on record which would otherwise be lost. Not for the first time self-criticism was expressed, but while doubts concerning self-importance and sell-out of friendship were not entirely banished, the view prevailed that the local witness needs to be put on paper. Scholarship is at work elsewhere; here a few appendices and footnotes are on offer. Auden's opinions on biographies of creative artists in general were, as Humphrey Carpenter[110] pointed out, highly contradictory. Again and again he said that the private life of poets and other people engaged in creative work is none of the public's business but he also said: "The biography of an artist, if his life as a whole was sufficiently interesting, is permissible, provided that the biographer and his readers realise that such an account throws no light whatsoever upon the artist's work." And "I do believe, however, that, more often than most people realise, his works may throw light upon his life." Carpenter's book calls itself "a first biography," and the author expressly restricts his aims: "It is not a work of literary criticism." It may also be felt to lack an analysis of some fundamental questions: about the depths of the poet's personality, his "otherness"

---

110 Humphrey Carpenter (1946–2005), English biographer, writer, and radio broadcaster best known for his biographies of Tolkien and other members of the literary society the Inklings.

(to confine this to his homosexuality would be to oversimplify), and the basis of his all-important relationship with Chester Kallman. As a starting point, "Early Auden," which presents and comments on the poetry, drama, and prose up to 1939, is most valuable, and Edward Mendelson will produce further works of scholarship.[111] What would Wystan Auden say if he could read *Auden in Love* by Chester's old college friend and last-minute stepmother Dorothy J. Farnon. In July 1985 the *Sunday Times* published a list of recommended holiday reading. The assessment of *Auden in Love* was a model of compression: "emetic but compulsive." I more than once came up against Auden's idée fixe about the irrelevance of the poet's private self, and asked him one day: "So no rotting apples in the desk drawer?" "No, no rotting apples." "And if you have an attack of the trots and interrupt your work?" "That would make no difference at all." Chester's sole explanation was that it was "a tick like any other," and that in any case he was totally inconsistent. Be that as it may, if the effect on the general public was judged as emetic, Auden's nausea can be imagined. All the same, it is a fascinating book, and for people who knew the two men only in the later years of their lives, does throw light on apparently conflicting phenomena and makes their actions, and Chester's character in particular, more comprehensible. When Auden first met Kallman he was just 32 and already a poet with an established reputation, respected and even revered on many a campus. Kallman was an 18 year old undergraduate, a brilliant, beautiful, focal point and leader of a crowd of young intellectuals of both sexes. He was a Dorian Grey figure, sparkling and

111 How right she was. By now almost the entire corpus of Auden's work has been brilliantly edited by Edward Mendelson, one of the greatest literary executors in the history of the role.

damned, hero and victim, immature and over-ripe, sensitive and heartless, a man capable of loving and of being loved but who was already—though Auden did not know it—addicted to promiscuity. In literature and music his knowledge was, for his age, above average, but when important examinations loomed a kind of petulant mood would come over him and he would fail to appear. Chester never wanted to earn his living, and all his life he was supported financially by other people, particularly by Auden. He usually promptly lost what he was given because he was perpetually being robbed by seamen picked up on the wharfs of New York. By one of them he was robbed of three months' income in succession. Or else he gave it away: no matter what actually happened, the money left his pocket. The scene shifts to a flat in the Esslingasse in Vienna's 3rd District, where Kallman once spent the winter. He gave a party one evening, and afterwards I took two or three of the men part of their way home in my car. When Chester told me later on that the man who, as it chanced, had been sitting beside me, had gone off with 2,000 schillings taken out of the pocket of a jacket hanging on the bedroom door, I could not know that this was not a mere incident but almost a matter of routine. When, ultimately, he took with him to Athens 80,000 sch. in cash (proceeds of the sale of a building plot) and lost it all on the way, this mishap was almost a foregone conclusion. That the sexual relationship between Auden and Kallman ceased as far back as 1941 is well known: from that time on—there is evidence in the poetry—sex and love became, for Auden, two separate matters.

He felt married to Chester (when he was not Mother) for the rest of his life, and he wrote that Chester was the only person who, emotionally and intellectually, was wholly indispensable to him. Like it or not, this statement has to be accepted with all the weight it carries. It was never possible, even in the Austrian era, to keep Chester in purdah for long, and when there was a visitor from Athens at Hinterholz 6 there could be tension. Auden gave orders to Yannis Boras in the abrupt tones of a colonial Englishman of yore speaking to the "boy," and when I asked one day at lunch: "Where is, er?" he said with a smirk of satisfaction: "I sent him up on to the roof to mend tiles." But fundamentally nothing had changed between them: this explains Auden's intense anxiety over the death of Boras in a car accident in Lower Austria, and his fear communicated itself to me as I searched for Chester in Vienna. It was nearly Christmas, what on earth would become of him, distraught and alone? (He had in fact not gone to Austria after all, but had not let Auden know.) There followed the gloomy summer of 1969 when Chester was sunk in deep depression while Wystan had a full work programme, and when he told me he could hardly think how Chester would get through the summer, this was indeed Mother speaking.

What was it in Chester Kallman that made him so entirely indispensable to Auden? Perhaps the question is impossible to answer; some may hold it to be inadmissible, or attempts to find points of reference impertinent. Others again may find the whole subject unappetising. But to anyone with an interest in psychology in the processes of creativity in general and in those of Auden in particular, there is no way of getting round this essential relationship. It may, after all, come to be seen as one of the most curious in the history of English literature. In their love of music, of opera above all, Kallman was in the lead. He was a minor poet who wrote because he needed to do so but his output was slight. Yet in many spheres which were of intense interest to Auden he had little, sometimes nothing to offer: German literature (though Chester picked up languages with uncommon facility; Wystan's spoken German was execrable but his comprehension unerring), the history of cultures, religion and liturgy, translation. When I was with them Wystan did not only most of the talking, but of the asking as well; his great charm lay in his alert interest in other people's work, and he would draw one out on the odder backwaters of Austrian history. This side of him comes out in a letter dated 6 July 1970. When Friedrich Heer and Auden, both entranced, struck sparks off one another all afternoon, Kallman was silent. Kallman lacked Auden's sensitivity to places and people, to the genius loci; perhaps it was just that he was an American, and a New Yorker, while Auden never lost his roots in Europe. On his own ground, operatic libretti, Chester Kallman was still in good running order, and when the *Rake's Progress* was put on in Vienna he wrote a letter to *Die Presse* protesting sharply against the cuts made by the producer. But of that conversational brilliance which old friends have described there was little sign. A scene comes to mind: Auden was away, and Chester asked me to meet him for lunch at a restaurant off the Kärntner-strasse. A young man whose background clearly lay somewhere within the crime belt near the Prater[112] was with him, and soon the youth and I were engrossed in conversation, while Chester, feeling out of it, sulked. Immediately after coffee it seemed best to leave them. Chester's intelligence and wit had not deserted him but they had too little scope, and, perhaps owing to his carp-like appearance, he was liable to be underestimated. He was good-natured, in course of time even affectionate, hospitable, and amusing. He looked after Auden

---

112 The Prater is a large public park in Vienna's Leopoldstadt district and includes the Wiener Riesenrad Ferris wheel; it figured prominently in the 1949 film *The Third Man*.

devotedly and we know that he was able to banish Auden's loneliness as no one else could. His misfortune was that he lacked those qualities which Auden possessed and which decide between success and failure. It cannot, all the same, have been easy living on a long-term basis with Auden in New York while attempting, even though fitfully, to develop his own personality and talents. Putting up with Auden's fads, his insistence on punctuality, and the rigid routine was one thing; to grow up, to mature in the shadow of this oversized tree was another. There was not enough light. So he fled, but without Mother there was no way he could live at all. It is essential, in the light of what happened later on, to remember Auden's generosity. His biographer mentioned the two boys whose further education was financed by Auden: I can confirm this as we lived next door to them for a few years. They were the sons of an artist; both made rapid careers in industrial management. But there were other examples. Wystan had telephoned and asked me to meet him and Chester at the Operncafé—the much-missed café-restaurant next to the Opera, now a car salesroom. They were waiting for Balanchine to join them after the performance, but we waited in vain and finally gave up and went home. There was a fourth at our table, a silent young man who, Chester said in an undertone, was a student of technology and Wystan was helping with his studies. It turned out that he lived not far from my flat so we drove off together, and he suddenly broke his silence to ask: "Who is this Professor Auden—is he well known?" There was a brief flurry after the 1968 uprising in Czechoslovakia. Towards the end of Auden's summer residence at 6 Kirchstetten the question cropped up whether he would be willing to lend the house to a Czech refugee and his wife. By mid-October Auden was in England.

(...)

Great generosity (these facts, even separately, are known to no more than two or three people) combined in Auden's character quite readily with his legendary stinginess in the small things of everyday life such as stamps or cigarettes. *Life* magazine, he told me one day with a beaming smile, had just paid him 5,000 dollars for an article. "I'm thinking of building on a dining room." "Very good idea," I said, "but for a start I shall smoke your cigarettes for the rest of the afternoon." I very much doubt whether I did. On the other hand he would order things to be sent out from Vienna without a second thought. After his car accident he sent me a message and I drove out to Kirchstetten. He was dishevelled and cross. It's a curious thing, he said, but the first chap who takes any notice of you when you're carried into hospital is not the doctor but the man from the accounts office who wants to know how you propose to pay for your treatment. No, he said, he didn't really need anything and Chester would arrive shortly, but he was running out of gin. If I'd be an angel and ring up Wild on the Neuer Markt and ask them to send a few bottles out—he told me the brand name—that would be splendid. When the friendly voice on the end of the line had repeated the order I asked when they would be making their next delivery in the area around Kirchstetten. "Oh but we never deliver out there," said the voice, "We make a special trip for the Herr Professor." Startled, I exclaimed, "For goodness' sake, that must cost him a packet—you can buy that brand of gin in Böheimkirchen!" "Certainly you can," said the voice which now sounded amused, "but why do we have to worry our heads over the way a Herr Professor flings his money around?" I liked the "we."

What was so American about the kitchen? When fitted kitchens first came in the Austrians called them "American" - the term is now as extinct as "Russian" tea but must still have been common parlance in Kirchstetten. There was a tidy line-up consisting of fridge, sink, low cupboards providing a good working surface, a corner cupboard the interior of which swung out, and a gas stove. Both men were very proud of the kitchen and it became Chester's habitat. But the whole point of a modern kitchen: the labour-saving working area, ample storage space, accessibility, was totally cancelled out by the permanent clutter. It was a matter of principle with Chester to have all cooking ingredients conveniently to hand, which meant that nothing was ever put away, and where his loving eye saw method, even the least fussy visitor could only see a shambles. But an interesting shambles owing to the exotic nature of the preserved foods and spices which Chester brought with him. There was for example a dried leaf which, detected by me in a casserole, was said to have no flavour but to serve as a stimulus or bridge to other flavours. It was clear from the beginning that the two of them were not so much drinking as eating their way into their graves owing to the enormous fat content of some of the dishes. I remember my horror as I watched a sauce being prepared in the mixer before it was re-heated to accompany the roast duck. It consisted of equal parts of rendered down duck fat and cream, and would have sustained a miner at the coal face for an indefinite period of time. If they could possibly help it, of course, neither Wystan nor Chester ever walked a yard.

Whether or not—and Chester was convinced that this was so—the business about alleged arrears of income tax shortened Auden's life must be left open. The "Declaration" to the tax authorities in which a great poet patiently explains how poetry comes to be written must be unique and deserves a place in the history of literature.

Declaration.[113]

Gentlemen,

My position is very simple: one pays income tax where one earns money, that is to say in my case, as a writer writing in English, in the United States and in England. In Austria I earn not one groschen, I merely spend schillings. You maintain that I possess a "material interest" in Austria, by which you presumably mean a "financial" interest. That might conceivably be the case if I had to say to myself: "I must go to Austria because I can only work in Austria!" But that is not the case. I have lived in many places in many different countries and was always able to work wherever I might be. I naturally have a "personal" interest in Austria, otherwise I should not come here. The landscape is pleasing, and I find the Austrians whose acquaintance I have made, friendly and charming. You say correctly that I once received an Austrian prize for literature. This was a great honour of which I am very proud. You cannot however seriously believe, Gentlemen, that I calculated: "If I continue to go to Austria maybe I shall be given a prize"? Until it was awarded to me I had never heard of this prize. It is equally clear that I cannot receive it a second time. You also go on to say that a road in Kirchstetten has been named Audenstraße after me. That was a very kind gesture on the part of the local council, but it cannot be maintained that I profit from it financially. Further, you say with truth that I have written several poems on Austrian themes. To this I would like to make three statements. I have never, in Austria, received so much as one penny for my poems. One or two of them have been translated into German, but

---

113 This is Auden's own text the one quoted above was Stella's translation from German.

in these cases the translators have received the money, not I. 2. I believe you are not clearly aware how poetry comes to be written. What is generally taken to be the subject matter is only a viewpoint, an occasion whereby certain thoughts about nature, God, history, mankind etc. may be expressed which the poet may have had in mind for a very long time. I wrote, for example, a poem to commemorate the 20th anniversary of the death of Josef Weinheber. Fundamentally however the poem is concerned with quite different things. First of all it is about the love which every poet, whatever his nationality, has for his mother tongue, and secondly about what happened after the war in the countries which were defeated, i.e. not only in Austria but in Germany and Italy. Again: in 1964 I wrote a poem with the title "Whitsunday in Kirchstetten" because it was where I happened to be. But the place is unimportant. In reality the question in this poem is what, for a Christian, is the meaning of the Feast of Pentecost. And this is valid for all countries in the same way. I believe you do not clearly recognize a poet's (Dichter) financial situation. If he is successful, a novelist can make a good deal of money. A poet (Lyriker) cannot, even if he is very well known, because he is only read by a minority. By far the greater part of my income comes not from the sale of my volumes of poetry but from book reviews, translations, lectures, etc., activities which have nothing to do with Austria. And while we are on the subject of translations you rightly say that I have a great interest in German and Austrian literature—I may add in music as well—but I do not have to come to Austria in order to read or to hear them. You see from all this that the arguments brought forward by you for subjecting me to payment of income tax are not valid. The most pertinent argument against it is that in the course of one year I always stay under six months in Austria and never spend more than three months here consecutively. A word in conclusion: if this in my view entirely unjustifiable nonsense does not cease, I shall leave Austria never to return, which would be very sad for me and perhaps too for the shopkeepers of Kirchstetten. One thing, Gentlemen, I cannot conceal from you: if this should happen it might give rise to a scandal of worldwide dimensions.

You ask why I have made over my half of our property in Kirchstetten to Mr. Chester Kallman who is not related to me. Mr. Kallman is my heir. I have no children and for years past he has been my literary collaborator. Jointly, we have written five new opera libretti, *The Rake's Progress, Elegy for Young Lovers, The Bassarids,* and *Love's Labours Lost.* And together we have made new translations of *The Magic Flute, Don Giovanni, Die Sieben Todsünden, Mahagonny,* and *Archifanfaro.* I am now 65 years old and must reckon with all eventualities such as a heart attack. As you know better than I, in the event of sudden death great difficulties arise for the heirs to landed property, particularly in a foreign country.

The German text was typed on a different machine, and the separate page joined to the Declaration.

Every day for the past year," said Chester, "I have stood outside his door in the early morning, afraid to go in." This was later. Now, Auden was dead, the voice issuing from the car radio had just said so. A few days ago we had talked about his reading in the Society for Literature on 28 September. Unfortunately, I said, I was obliged to drive to Linz and to spend the night there, but they were welcome to use my Vienna flat. It was maddening and I would just as soon put it off. No, said Auden, mustn't do that, one should stick to one's commitments. "And you won't be missing much," he reassured me, "you've heard it all before." We would meet again in a few

days' time and then he would tell me all about it. He was not
sure about the flat but he would let me know in good time.
On 24 September he wrote a note to say that he did not need
the flat, he would go to the Hotel Altenburgerhof. The handwriting is ragged. Linz already lay far behind, the car radio
went on muttering to itself unheeded until the familiar voice
of Friedrich Heer came through, reading one of his book reviews. It was consoling in a world where, suddenly, a signpost was missing. What are you howling about, I asked myself, what gives you the right to mourn for Wystan? Think
of Chester. It was impossible not to think of Chester: it was
not so much a question how much he would grieve over the
death of Wystan, as how he would survive at all. Leaving the
autobahn at St. Pölten I drove straight to Kirchstetten; it
seemed to be just possible that he might have arrived in the
meantime. But the green shutters were closed and there was
no one about apart from the wall-eyed dog, an exceptionally hideous mongrel belonging to Frau Strobl, which barked
in an irritating falsetto. He barked from a position close beside me while I wrote a note and stuck it in the chink between the door's shutters, and he was still barking as I shut
the garden gate behind me. The answer to my note was a telephone call from Frau Strobl: Herr Kallman said, would I come
over to tea the next day? That was the Sunday. The sitting
room seemed to be full of people. Chester was sitting on the
corner-seat facing the door, where Auden always used to sit,
every chair appeared to be occupied and two young men were
sitting on the floor. Chester hurried across the room, hugged
me and said "The whole thing's terrible, you have to help me."
I was introduced to the others. Mrs. Thekla Clark and her
daughter had come up from Florence as soon as they heard
the news; there was Frau Maria Seitz, headmistress of the
high school; Herr Enzinger, the mayor of Kirchstetten,

the film scriptwriter Adolf Opel, and the young men. Clearly, the meeting to discuss the funeral arrangements was not proceeding smoothly. The mayor looked annoyed, Frau Seitz looked worried, and Mrs Clark bewildered. There were, of course, language difficulties. Mayor Enzinger spoke not a word of English and the Clarks no German, while the headmistress had a certain command of English but did not feel up to acting as interpreter and adviser in one; Chester's German was perfectly adequate. The root of the problem lay on a deeper level, where two separate cultures collided head on. Chester was barely coherent, but he managed to explain his point of view. He loathed, from the bottom of his heart everything in the way of *pompes funèbres*. He wanted to bury Auden, he said, quietly and privately and, if it could possibly be managed, on Tuesday. He had already informed Wystan's brother Dr. John Auden, Stephen Spender, and others of the arrangements and asked them to arrive, if not tomorrow, then on Tuesday morning at the latest. On the other hand the mayor of Kirchstetten, he went on, wanted to lay on a really big show with brass bands and all the rest of it, and what was more on the Saturday to give as many people as possible the chance to come. The Ministry of Education and the provincial council of Lower Austria were to be represented, and as the last straw the hearse was to drive up to the house. He would not allow any of this, he said: "I can't bear it and I won't have it." Mayor Enzinger drew a deep breath. The first thing we had to realise, he pointed out, was that the body had not yet been released by the authorities. In all cases where the cause of death is not wholly clear certain formalities are obligatory, and even intervention at a high level would not work miracles. Everything takes time. And how could anyone expect it of him, the Bürgermeister, that he should refrain from notifying the Ministry and the Cultural depart-

ment of the Council of the death of Professor Auden? It was
as much as his job was worth. Now Frau Seitz spoke. The inhabitants of Kirchstetten, she believed, would hardly bury
a dog in the manner proposed by Herr Kallman, let alone
a great poet. Chester Kallman's position was entirely comprehensible—to some of us. To him, an American of Jewish
origin and a non-believer, the whole pomp and circumstance
of a traditional Austrian funeral was abhorrent. Where prominent personages are concerned, there would certainly be
the local brass band, and where appropriate delegations representing the voluntary fire brigade, the federal railways, the
veterans' association and others besides, and the gamekeepers would blow their horns and wish him good hunting in
the Elysian fields. To Chester's mind such folksy rituals were
as foreign as the burial rites of the Incas. He did not know
that not very long ago in Lower Austria, Auden as a bachelor would have been accompanied in the funeral procession
by a "bride" dressed in white. He was unable to understand
that his intentions were an intolerable affront to the population of Kirchstetten. In his despair, it certainly never occurred to him that Auden himself would very likely have
been entranced at the idea of a slap-up funeral with all the
trimmings—one can almost hear his Olympian laughter—
followed by a hearty meal at the inn where he had so often
had his lunch. As it turned out, Chester got no marks in local opinion for this finale either, as the meal consisted of
Leberkäs with vegetables: This consisted of fried slices off
a loaf of a flabby substance which is neither liver nor cheese
related to the Frankfurter sausage. It is a homely, juicy meal
all too familiar to every Austrian; and it is cheap. There
would be much talk of this also after all was over. For their
part, the local people were forgetting that Chester was probably in financial straits—not that this would have been tak-

en as an excuse. For a moment the discussion had come to a standstill. The young men who took no part in it and conversed in whispers, fetched more beer, Frau Strobl walked in and out and rolled a baleful eye on us as she spoke into Chester's ear. The points at issue were not only When and How Much; there was also the matter of the church service and the prayers at the graveside. Many people in Austria had assumed Auden to be of the Roman Catholic faith; he had of course remained a member of the Anglican and Episcopalian churches. The misunderstanding arose from his regular attendance at mass in the parish church and his friendly relationship with Father Lustkandl, the parish priest referred to in "Whitsunday in Kirchstetten." Auden asked Lustkandl's sucessor for permission to be buried in the churchyard, and his wish was acceded to. Evidently, the next logical thing to do, then, was to approach the chaplain to the British Embassy in Vienna, the Revd. Bruce Duncan, and ask him to officiate. What form of service this should be—there could be no question of a funeral mass—left everyone present at a loss. We agreed at last that it ought to be some kind of ecumenical ceremony held jointly by the two clergymen, but that first of all, the plan must be put before Dr. John Auden. At this juncture Chester Kallman withdrew his insistence on the impossibly early date for the funeral. The room had become much too warm, the oxygen was running out, and Chester would not be able to stand much more pressure. The most urgent objective was quite simply to free him from our burdensome presence. Once everyone had agreed that Auden's relations must be told immediately that the funeral had been postponed, the moment had come to dissolve the meeting. Mrs. Clark undertook to telephone to London and Frau Strobl would drive her to the Post Office. Chester asked me to talk everything over with Frau Seitz and Herr Enzinger and reach definite conclusions. We all stood up, Chester came across the room to me and spoke in an undertone. He was completely exhausted, he said, he couldn't stand much more. "I'll do anything you want, you must just try to hold the others in check." Finally he said "It'll be all right, I'm crammed full of tranquillizers, all I need is a bit of a rest." He embraced me warmly and left the room. (...)

At the lowest point in Kirchstetten where the roads divide the procession halted while the coffin was transferred from the hearse to a hand-drawn bier. At this point the Church took charge and the procession resumed its steady pace; photographs exist which were taken during the brief interval. To British ears quite unremarkable, the ecumenical service was much talked about in Austrian circles because nothing of the kind had been known before. The Revd. Bruce Duncan, today Rector of Crediton in Devon, can remember little about the general circumstances but confirms that he used the Book of Common Prayer and the long reading from the first Letter of St. Paul to the Corinthians, chapter 15, verses 20-58. Beyond that, all he recalls is his difficulties with Chester.

Reaching for my Authorised Version, for surely no one would have dared to use any other, on second thoughts I also took out the New Testament as translated into German by Martin Luther. After reading the English text through very slowly, and then a second time, I did the same with the Lutheran Bible and, lost in thought, compared the two, verse by verse.

"How nice to see you," said Auden who was sitting on one of the white garden chairs with the red covers, "it's a bit *einsam* here. And I wanted to write and tell you that the technical word for buddle is *Erzwaschtrog*. I hope there is an equivalent German euphemism for "senior citizen." Oh and adit is *Stollen*, and although I may be wrong, I guess concentrating mill is *Vereinigungsmühle*." "What a mercy you've told me," I said, relieved. "I should have to have dug up such frightful words in the British Council library. But do you think people will understand all that about the primary and secondary worlds, or will they get muddled?" "It's perfectly simple," said Auden. "The initial impulse to create a secondary world is a feeling of awe aroused by encounters, in the primary world, with sacred beings or events." "There is one glory of the sun," I heard myself say, "and another glory of the moon, and another glory of the stars: for on star differeth from another in glory." "Ah," he said, "you've been reading Corinthians One, chapter 15. 'Let us eat and drink; for tomorrow we die.' Chester and I took that bidding rather too literally." "Who would know where that familiar quotation comes from?" I wondered. "I would," said Auden. "I've been looking up the German text. Have you ever compared the Authorized Version with Martin Luther?" "Funny you should ask that," I said. "It's one of the things I forgot to talk to you about. 'Be not deceived: evil communications corrupt good manners.' He renders that as *Lasset euch nicht verführen! Böse Geschwätze verderben gute Sitten*." "Very neat," said Auden happily. "I like 'evil chatter' better than 'communications'." "The publishers," I said, "have a rather heavy-handed way of printing the more quotable bits in bold-face. But in the next verse Luther seems to flounder. '*Werdet doch einmal recht nüchtern und sündiget nicht!*' 'Do be a bit sober for once,' he pleads. 'And sin not.' King James's translators fancied that St Paul cried out 'Awake to righteousness!'" "Who knows what he really said." "Luther's language is very fine as he reaches the climax: '*Siehe, ich sage euch ein Geheimnis...*'" But Auden was speaking. "Behold, I shew you a mystery: we shall not all sleep, but we shall all be changed. In a moment, in the twinkling of an eye, at the last trump: for the trumpet shall sound, and the dead shall be raised incorruptible, and we shall be changed.'" And with that he vanished. Now wide awake, I put the two books back on their shelf and settled down to re-type Auden's speech at Neulengbach. *"Sehr verehrter Herr Landeshauptmann*, Ladies and gentlemen: I hope you will pardon me if I speak somewhat personally. I do so, not out of vanity..."

Envelope of a letter from Auden to Stella

Auden's Letters

28 April 1965

JOSEPH WEINHEBER
(1892–1945)
Reaching my gate a narrow
Lane from the village
Passes on into a wood:
When I walk that way,
It seems befitting to stop
And look through the fence
Of your garden where (under
The circs they had to)
They buried you like a loved
Old family dog.

Categorised enemies
Twenty years ago,
Now next-door neighbors, we might
Have become good friends,
Sharing a common ambit
And love of the word,
Over a golden *Kremser*
Had many a long
Language on syntax, commas,
Versification.

Yes, yes, it has to be said:
Men of great damage
And malengine took you up.
Did they for long, though,

Take you in, who to Goebbels'
Offer of culture
Countered *In Ruah lassen*!?
But Rag, Tag, Bobtail
Prefer a stink, and the young
Condemn you unread.

What, had you ever heard of etc

Wednesday. Kirchstetten

Dear Stella:
Many thanks for your letter. Will try and call you today by phone. I enclose a prose translation made by me and
a German friend; Since the copy I sent you, I have made a few
slight changes in stanza 3. (see above) Could you check the
translation for errors.
Love
Wystan.

Feb 3rd, 1966

Dear Stella,

Many thanks for your nice long letter. Stephen has a genius for subtle misrepresentation. "Serious insistence on unseriousness" telescopes two distinct convictions of mine, falsifying both.

1) I believe it to be a serious moral error when an artist overestimates the importance of art and, by implication, of himself. One must admit that the political history of Europe, with the same horrors, would be what it has been, if Dante, Shakespeare, Goethe,

Titian, Mozart, et al, had never existed.

2) I believe that the only way in which, to-day at any rate, one can speak seriously about serious matters (the alternative is silence) is comically. I am surprised to hear from you that Jews find this hard to accept. I have enormously admired—and been influenced by—the tradition of Jewish humor. More than any other people, surely, they have seen in serious matters, that is to say, human suffering, the contradictions of human existence, and the relation between man and God, occasions for humorous expression, e.g.: "If the rich could hire other people to die for them, the poor could make a wonderful living," or "Truth rests with God alone, and a little bit with me," or "God will provide—ah, if only He would till He does so." So! You encountered the one-whose-name-we-never-mention. Why Chester should have been so foolish as to invite him to a party, I cannot imagine. If he is to be seen at all, he must be seen alone. Incidentally, next time you see Chester, scold him a) for not writing to me b) for not answering Harrison's cable. All well here except for a leaking kitchen roof. No doubt you read about our Black-

Out and Transit Strike. (My typewriter is on the blink, hence the hiatuses.) A friend of mine who teaches schyzophrenics, [sic] has a seventeen-year-old girl who is interested in poetry. Asked what poets she liked, she mentioned me. "I happen to know him quite well," said my friend. To which the girl in astonishment: "You mean to say, he's still alive!" Expect to get back to Kirchstetten about April 20th.

much love and greetings to son and mum-in-law

Wystan.

77 St Mark's Place
New York City

New York 10003
Nov 8th 1966

Dear Stella,

A disaster has happened. Frau Eiermann died of a heart-attack on Nov 4th. (Have just heard this from my lawyer.). A minor worry connected with this is what is happening to her cats and ours. I suppose they will probably have to be destroyed. Next time you are travelling between Fridau and Wien, could you be a dear and stop in Kirchstetten to see what is happening. Incidentally, in case you should need it my lawyer's name and address is Dr. Walter Redlich. Wien I. Wipplingerstrasse, 24-26. Canterbury was quite fun. The Archbishop came to my first lecture.

Love
Wystan

4 October 1968

[From his Kirchstetten address as per reverse of the envelope. Included [a] typescript of his poem August 1968]

AUGUST 1968
The ogre does what ogres can,
Deeds quite impossible for man,
but one prize is beyond his reach:
The ogre cannot master Speech.
About a subjugated plain,
Among its desperate and slain,
The ogre stalks with hands on hips,
While drivel gushes from his lips.

Dear Stella,

Terribly sorry about last Sunday. Since I had no idea when we should be able to get to you, I thought it was unfair to the kitchen not to cancel. Have a nice winter and will see you, I hope, early in April.

Love

Wystan

Dec 13th 1968

St Mark's Place
New York City
N.Y. 10003

Dear Stella:

Chester has just telephoned me from Athens to say that
his Greek friend Jean Boras, whom I think you have met,
while driving my car between Vienna and Kirchstetten coll-
eded [sic] with a Lastwagen and was killed. Chester is going
to Vienna, but he was too upset for me to find out where he
would stay. I presume in Kirchstetten. If you can get in touch
him and help him in any way (there are purely practical matters to be considered, like the car-papers and insurance policy) I should be most grateful,

Love
Wystan

Dear Stella:

I am in despair. I wrote to my lawyer and to our factotum,
Otto Holfmann to find out details about the accident and the
whereabouts and condition of the car, but have not heard
a word. Chester postpones his visit to Vienna and I don't
know his plans. Could you possibly ring Holfmann to see if
he knows anything.

Address. Wien VII, Schweighofergasse 4/21
Tel : 93/88/155. .
The Registration Number of my car is W. 618-948.
Love
Wystan.

Jan 4th 1969
77 St Mark's Place
New York City
New York 10003
U.S.A.
Jan 4th

Dear Stella,

Many thanks for your letter. I gather that, in the end, Chester decided not to go to Vienna. Meanwhile, I am in despair about the practical matter of the whereabouts and condition of the car. No answer from Holfman [sic]. Can he be dead, too? I should be most grateful if you would call him or on him. to find out what is the matter. Among other things he has the cheques for my Hausmeisterin.

Address Otto Hoffmann. Wien VII. Karl Schweighofegasse 4/21. Tel. 93/88/155.

I hear that my old lawyer is supervising the case but have till now heard nothing from him. Again could you call him for me.

Dr Walter Redlich. Wien XIX . Paradisgasse 55. Tel: 36/43/83.

Terribly sorry to be such a nuisance, but I don't know what to do. I can't get in touch with the Insurance till I know more.

love
Wystan

May 21st. 1970

Dear Stella,

You're an angel. I have to deliver this in Neulengbach on Sunday, June 14th. In case your dictionary doesn't give it, the German for the technical word buddle (page 1, near the bottom) is *Erzwaschtrog*. I hope there is an equivalent German euphemism for "the Senior Citizen." If there is a special honorary title of address for a *Landeshauptman*, please supply.

Love

Wystan

FREEDOM AND NECESSITY IN THE ARTS

Sehr veehrter Herr Landeshauptmann, meine Damen und Herren:

I hope you will pardon me if I speak somewhat personally. I do so, not out of vanity, but because I do not wish to give the impression that I am attempting to lay down absolute laws which are valid for all. I give you my experiences as a poet, in the hope that you will be able to compare them with yours, and form your own judgment about them. Most of what I know about the writing of poetry, or at least about the kind I am interested in writing, I discovered long before I took any interest in poetry itself.

Between the ages of six and twelve, I spent a great many of my waking hours in the fabrication of a private secondary sacred world, the basic elements of which were a) a limestone landscape mainly derived from the Pennine Moors in the North of England and b) an industry—lead-mining. It is no doubt psychologically significant that my sacred world was autistic—that is to say, I had no wish to share it with others nor could I have done so. However, though constructed for and inhabited by myself alone, I needed the help of others, my parents in particular, in collecting its basic materials; others had to procure for me the necessary text-books on geology and machinery, maps, catalogues, guide-books, and photographs and when occasion offered to take me down real mines, tasks which they performed with unfailing patience and generosity.

From this activity, I learned certain principles which I was later to find applied to all artistic fabrication. First, whatever other elements it may include, the initial impulse to create a secondary world is a feeling of awe aroused by encounters, in the Primary World, with sacred beings or events. This feeling of awe is an imperative, that is to say one is not free to choose the object or the event that arouses it. Though every work of art is a secondary world, it cannot be constructed *ex nihilo*, but is a selection from and a recombination of the contents of the Primary World. Even the "purest" poem, in the French Symboliste sense, is made of words which are not the poet's private property, but the communal creation of the linguistic group to whom he belongs, so that their meaning can be looked up in a dictionary.

Secondly, in constructing my private world, I discovered that, though this was a game, or rather precisely *because it was a game*—that is to say, not a necessity like eating or sleeping, but something I was free to do or not as I chose—it could not be played without rules. Absolute freedom is meaningless: freedom can only be realised in a choice between alternatives. A secondary world, be it a poem, or a game of football or bridge, must be as much a world of law as the Primary, the only difference being that in the world of games one is free to decide what its laws shall be. But to all games as to real life, Goethe's lines apply.

In der Beschränkung zeigt sich erst der Meister,
Und das Gesetz nur kann uns Freiheit geben.

As regards my particular lead-mining world, I decided, or rather, without conscious decision, I instinctively felt that I must impose two restrictions upon my freedom of fantasy. In choosing what objects were to be included, I was free to select this and reject that, on condition that both were real objects in the Primary World, to choose, for example, between two kinds of water-turbine, which could be found in a text-book on mining machinery or a manufacturer's catalogue: but I was not free to invent one. In deciding how my world was to function, I could choose between two practical possibilities—a mine can be drained either by an adit or a pump but physical impossibilities and magic means were forbidden. When I say forbidden, I mean that I felt, in some obscure way, that they were morally forbidden.

Then there came a day when the moral issue became quite conscious. As I was planning my Platonic Idea of a concentrating-mill, I ran into difficulties. I had to choose between two types of a certain machine for separating the slimes, called a buddle. One type I found more sacred or "beautiful," but the other type was, I knew from my reading, the more efficient. At this point I realised that it was my moral duty to sacrifice my aesthetic preference to reality or truth. when, later, I began to write poetry, I found that, for me, at least, the same obligation was binding. That is to say, I cannot accept the doctrine that, in poetry, there is a "suspension of belief." A poet must never make a statement simply because it sounds poetically exciting: he must also believe it to be true. This does not mean, of course, that one can only appreciate a poet whose beliefs happen to coincide with one's own. It does mean, however, that one must be convinced that the poet really believes what he says, however odd the belief may seem to oneself. Between constructing a private fantasy world for oneself alone and writing poetry, there is, of course, a profound difference.

A fantasy world exists only in the head of its creator: a poem is a public verbal object intended to be read and enjoyed by others. To become conscious of others is to become conscious of historical time in various ways. The contents of a poem are necessarily past experiences, and the goal of a poem is necessarily in the future, since it cannot be read until it has been written. Again, to write a poem is to engage in an activity which human beings have practised for centuries.

If one asks why human beings make poems or paint pictures or compose music, I can see two possible answers. Firstly all the artistic media are forms of an activity peculiar to human beings, namely, Personal Speech. Many animals have impersonal codes of communications, visual, olfactory, auditory signals, by which they convey to other members of their species vital information about food, territory, sex, the presence of enemies, etc., and in social animals like the bee, such a code may be exceedingly complex. We, too, of course, often use words in the same way, as when I ask a stranger the way to the railroad station. But when we truly speak, we do something quite different. We speak as person to person in order to disclose ourselves to others and share our experiences with them, not because we must, but because we enjoy doing so. This activity is sometimes quite erroneously called "self-expression." If I write a poem about experiences I have had, I do so because I think it should be of interest and value to others: the fact that it has till now only been my experience is accidental. What the poet or any artist has to convey is a perception of a reality common to all, but seen from a unique perspective, which it is his duty as well as his pleasure to share with others. To small truths as well as great, St. Augustine's words apply.

The truth is neither mine nor his nor another's; but belongs to us all whom Thou callest to partake of it: warning us terribly, not to account it private to ourselves, lest we be deprived of it. Then the second impulse to artistic fabrication is the desire to transcend our mortality, by making objects which, unlike ourselves, are not subject to natural death, but can remain permanently "on hand" in the world, long after we and our society have perished. Every genuine work of art, I believe, exhibits two qualities, Nowness and Permanence. By Nowness I mean the quality which enables an art historian to date a work, at least, approximately. If, for example, one listens to a composition by Palestrina and one by Mozart, one knows immediately that, quite aside from their artistic merits, Palestrina must have lived earlier than Mozart: he could not possibly have written as he did after Mozart. By Permanence, I mean that the work continues to have relevance and importance long after its creator is dead. In the history of Art, unlike the history of Science, no genuine work of art is made obsolete by a later work. Past science is of interest only to the historian of science, not to what scientists are doing at this moment.

Past works of art, on the other hand, are of the utmost importance to the contemporary practitioner. Every artist tries to produce something new, but in the hope that, in time, it will take its proper place in the tradition of his art. And he cannot produce anything significantly original unless he knows well what has already been done; that is to say, he cannot "rebel" against the past without having a profound reverence for it. There are periods in history when the arts develop uninterruptedly, each generation building on the achievements of the previous generation. There are other periods when radical breaks seem to be necessary. However, when they are, one will generally find that the "radical" artist does not disown the past, but finds in works of a much earlier period or in those of culture than his own, the clue as to what he should do now. In my own case, for example, I know how much I owe to Anglo-Saxon and Medieval Poetry. When I review the contemporary artistic scene, it strikes me how extraordinarily fortunate men like Stravinsky, Picasso, Eliot, etc., that is, those persons we think of as the founders of "modern" art, were in being born when they were, so that they came to manhood before 1914. Until the First World War, western society was still pretty much what it had been in the nineteenth century. This meant that for these artists, the felt need to create something new arose from an artistic imperative, not a historic imperative. No one asked himself: "What is the proper kind of music to compose or picture to paint or poem to write in the year 1912?" Secondly, their contemporary audiences were mostly conservative, but honestly so. Those, for instance, who were scandalised by Le Sacre du Printemps, may seem to us now to have been old fogies, but their reaction was genuine. They did not say to themselves: "Times have changed and we must change with them in order not to be left behind." Here are a few statements by Stravinsky to which the young, whether artists or critics would do well to listen and ponder over.

In my youth the new music grew out of, and in reaction to, traditions, whereas it appears to be evolving to-day as much from social needs as interior artistic ones... The status of new music as a category is another incomparable. It had none at all in my early years, being in fact categorically opposed, and often with real hostility. But the unsuccess of composers of my generation at least kept them from trading on success, and our unsuccess may have been less insidious than the automatic superlatives which nowadays kill the new by absorbing it to death.

* * *

The use of the new hardware naturally appears to the new musician as "historically imperative"; but music is made out of musical imperatives, and the awareness of historical processes is probably best left to future and different kinds of wage-earners.

* * *

In times, like our own, of rapid social change and political crisis, there is always a danger of confusing the principles governing political action and those governing artistic fabrication. The most important of such confusions are three. Firstly, one may come to think of artistic fabrication as a form of political action. Every citizen, poets included, has a duty to be politically "engagé," that is, to play a responsible part in seeing that the society of which he is a member shall function properly and improve. But the poet, *qua* poet, has only one political function. Since language is his medium, it is his duty, by his own example, to defend his mother-tongue against corruption by demagogues, journalists, the mass-media etc. As Karl Kraus said: *Die Sprache ist die, Mutter, nicht das Magd, des Gedankens*, and when language loses its meaning, its place is taken by violence. Of course, the poet may use political and social events as subject-matter for poems—they are as much a part of human experience as love or nature—but he must never imagine that his poems have the power to affect the course of history. The political and social history of Europe would be what it has been if Dante, Shakespeare, Goethe, Michael Angelo, Titian, Mozart, Beethoven, etc., had never existed. Where political and social evils are concerned, only two things are effective: political action and straightforward, truthful, detailed journalistic rapportage of the facts. The Arts are powerless. The second confusion, of which Plato is the most famous example, is to take artistic fabrication as the model for a good society. Such a model, if put into practice, is bound to produce a tyranny. The aim of the artist is to produce an object which is complete and will endure without change. In the "city" of a poem, there are always the same inhabitants doing exactly the same jobs forever. A society which was really like a good poem, embodying the aesthetic virtues of order, economy, and subordination of the detail to the whole, would be a nightmare of horror for, given the historical reality of actual men, such a society could only come into being through selective breeding, extermination of the physically and mentally unfit, absolute obedience to its director, a large slave class kept out of sight in cellars strictest censorship of the Arts, forbidding anything to be said which is out of keeping with the official "line." The third confusion, typical of our western "free" societies at this time, is the opposite of Plato's, namely to take political action as the model for artistic fabrication. Political action is a necessity, that is to say, at the very moment something has to be done, and it is momentary—action at this moment is immediately followed by another action at the next. Artistic fabrication, on the other hand, is voluntary—the alternative to one work of art can be no work of art—and the artistic object is permanent, that is to say, immune to historical change. The attempt to model artistic fabrication on political action can, therefore, only reduce it to momentary and arbitrary "happenings," a conformism with the tyranny of the immediate moment which is far more enslaving and destructive of integrity than any conformism with past tradition.

What then, can the Arts do for us? In my opinion, they can do two things. They can, as Dr. Johnson said, "enable us a little better to enjoy life or a little better to endure it." And, because they are objects permanently on hand in the world, they are the chief means by which the living are able to break bread with the dead, and, without a communication with the dead, I do not believe that a fully human civilised life is possible. Perhaps, too, in our age, the mere making of a work of art is itself a political act. So long as artists exist, making what they please or think they ought to make, even if their works are not terribly good, they remind the Management of something managers need to be reminded of, namely, that the managed are people with faces, not anonymous numbers, that *Homo Laborans* is also *Homo Ludens*. And now, I hope those of you who know no English will forgive me if I conclude these remarks with a light poem of my own, entitled Doggerel by a Senior Citizen.

> Our earth in 1969
> Is not the planet I call mine,
> The world, I mean, that gives me strength
> To hold off chaos at arm's length.
>
> My Eden landscapes and their climes
> Are constructs from Edwardian times,
> When bath-rooms took up lots of space,
> And, before eating, one said Grace.
>
> The automobile, the aeroplane,
> Are useful gadgets, but profane:
> The enginry of which I dream
> Is moved by water or by steam.
>
> Reason requires that I approve
> The light-bulb which I cannot love:
> To me more reverence-commanding
> A fish-tail burner on the landing.

My family ghosts I fought and routed,
Their values, though, I never doubted:
I thought the Protestant Work—Ethic
Both practical and sympathetic.

When couples played or sang duets,
It was immoral to have debts:
I shall continue till I die
To pay in cash for what I buy.

The Book of Common Prayer we knew
Was that of 1662:
Though with—it sermons may be well,
Liturgical reforms are hell.

Sex was of course—it always is —
The most enticing of mysteries,
But news-stands did not then supply
Manichean pornography.

Then Speech was mannerly, an Art,
Like learning not to belch or fart:
I cannot settle which is worse,
The Anti-Novel or Free Verse.

Nor are those Ph.D's my kith,
Who dig the symbol and the myth:
I count myself a man of letters
Who writes, or hopes to, for his betters.

Dare any call Permissiveness
An educational success?

Saner those class-rooms which I sat in,
Compelled to study Greek and Latin.

Though I suspect the term is crap,
There is a Generation Gap,
Who is to blame? Those, old or young,
Who will not learn their Mother-Tongue.

But Love, at least, is not a state
Either en vogue or out-of-date,
And I've true friends, I will allow,
To talk and eat with here and now.

Me alienated? Bosh! It's just
As a sworn citizen who must
Skirmish with it that I feel
Most at home with what is Real.

At this point, a little digression on the subject of "free"
verse, which seems now to be almost universal among young
poets. Though excellent examples, the poems of D.H. Law-
rence, for example, exist, they are, in my opinion, the excep-
tion, not the rule. The great virtue of formal metrical rules
is that they forbid automatic responses and, by forcing the
poet to have second thoughts, free him from the fetters of
self. All too often, the result of not having a fixed form to
be true to is a self-indulgence which in the detached reader can only cause boredom. Further, in my experience, contrary to what one might expect, the free-verse poets sound
much more like each other than those who write in fixed
forms. Whatever freedom may do, it does not, it would seem,
make for originality.

6 July 19
3062 KIRCHSTETTEN
BEZ. ST. PÖLTEN
HINTERHOLZ 6
N.-Ö., AUSTRIA

Dear Stella,

Have just finished reading *Austria* by which I was enchanted as well as instructed. My! How erudite you are. Where did
you dig up all those stories? A trifle alarmed that it may at-
tract more tourists, which I'm sure you don't welcome any
more than I do. (Thanks, by the way, for the reference to my
garage.). Am very curious to learn more about *The Life and Adventures of Peter Prosch*. Is it in print? Shouldn't it be translated? As you say, the relation between art and society is very
odd. Why should the Vienna of 1890-1918 have produced
such a florescence? (Chester can appreciate Bruckner better
than I). Even odder to me is the Biedermayer [sic] period. No
one can possibly approve of Metternich's police state, yet, in
a more liberal milieu, could Stifter, Raimund, Nestroy, have
written what they did? Hope this reaches you. Looking forward to seeing you in Sept.

Love and admiration
Wystan

Oct 19th 1971
Spender
15 Loudoun Rd
London. N.W.8

Dear Stella,

Were very disappointed that we didn't see you again before we left. You seem to have stayed in England much lon-
ger than usual. This morning a copy of *Austria* arrived from
Faber's: The illustrations, which I hadn't seen before, seem
excellent. Overleaf a poem I want to dedicate to you. Firstly, because of its subject and, secondly, because it is written
in an imitation of a medieval Welsh metre called a Cywydd.
Return to New York on Nov 1st.

    Love
Wystan

STARK BEWÖLKT
(*for Stella Musulin*)

I'm no photophil who burns
his body brown on beaches:
foolish I find this fashion
of modern surf-riding man.
Let plants by all means sun-bathe,
it helps them to make their meals:
exposure, though, to ultra-
violet vapids the brain,
bids us be stodge and stupid.
Still, safe in some sheltered shade,

or watching through a window,
an ageing male, I demand
to see a shining summer,
a sky bright and wholly blue,
save for a drifting cloudlet
like a dollop of whipped cream.
This year all is unthuswise:
O why so glum, weather-god?

Day after day we waken
to be scolded by a scowl,
venomous and vindictive,
a flat frowning Friday face,
horrid as a hang-over,
and mean as well: if you must
so disarray the heavens,
at least you might let them rain.
(Water is always welcome
for trees to take neat and men
to make brandy or beer with.)
But, no, we don't get a drop:
dry you remain and doleful
in a perpetual pique.

Fowls mope, flowers are wretched,
the raspberry-canes are forced
into phyllomania:
to ignore you, not be cross,
one would have to be either
drunk, lit on amphetamines,
or a feverish lover.
Being dead sober all day,
I find your bearing boorish,

by four in the afternoon
frequently close the curtains
to shut your shabbiness out.

Who or what are you mad at?
What has poor Austria done
to draw such disapproval?
The *Beamterei*, it's true,
is as awful as ever,
the drivers are dangerous,
standards at the *Staatsoper*
steadily decline each year,
and *Wien's* become provincial
compared to the pride she was.
Still, it's a cosy country,
unracked by riots or strikes
and backward at drug-taking:
I've heard of a dozen lands
where life sounds far more ugsome,
fitter goals for your disgust.
(I needn't name them, for you, whose
glance circumspects the whole globe,
ken at first hand what's cooking.)

Have done! What good does it do,
dumb god, just to deject us?
Foul our function may be, but
foul weather won't reform it.
If you merely wish our world
to mend its ways, remember:
when happy, men on the whole
behave a wee bit better,
when unhappy, always worse.

Feb 22nd, 1972

77 St Mark's Place
New York City
N.Y. 10003

Dear Stella;

Many thanks for your letter. Whatever made you imagine I was quitting Kirchstetten? Of course I'm not. The change is that I shall be spending my winters in Oxford, not in New York.

Love

· Wystan

3062 KIRCHSTETTEN
BEZ. ST. PÖLTEN
HINTERHOLZ 6
N.-Ö., AUSTRIA
Sept 24th 1973

Dear Stella,

I don't yet know at what time the reading is to be. If not until 8 p.m. I shall eat first, because I like to go to bed early. Many thanks for the invitation to stay the night with you, but I have already booked a room at the Hotel Hof [sic] Altburgenhof,

love
Wystan

And it was at the Hotel Altenburgerhof that Auden died on September 29 1973. He asked to be driven to the hotel in "a nice car," which was an unusual request for him. When Chester found him in the morning he told friends "I knew he was dead. He was lying on his right-hand side. Wystan never slept on his right-hand side."

Photo Credits

Unless otherwise noted, the photos are from Stella Musulin's or from the Author's collection. Every effort has been made to identify copyright holders and obtain their permission for the use of copyright material. Notification of any additions or corrections that should be incorporated in future reprints or editions of this book would be greatly appreciated.

p. 15. Alan Ansen. Photo by Judith Moffett. Source: https://commons.wikimedia.org/wiki/File:AlanAnsen1973.jpg.

p. 20. Hotel Altenburgerhof Vienna where Auden died. Source: https://www.geschichtewiki.wien.gv.at/Datei:Walfischgasse5.jpg.

p. 32. Auden's grave in the churchyard at Kirchstetten. Source: Wikimedia Commons, https://commons.wikimedia.org/wiki/File:Auden%27s_grave.JPG.

p. 42. Maria Sense, owner of Bar Maria in Forio, with Auden. Photo by Liza Meyerlist. Staatsarchiv des Kantons Luzern, https://memobase.ch/de/object/akl-002-1702413.

p. 45. Anthony Hecht at the Iowa Writer's Workshop in 1947. Source: Wikimedia Commons, https://commons.wikimedia.org/wiki/File:Antony_Hecht_1947.jpg.

p. 47. Putridarium, Castello Aragonese, Ischia. Source: Wikimedia Commons, https://commons.wikimedia.org/wiki/File:Ischia,_castello_aragonese,_cimitero_delle_clarisse,_con_scolatoi_%28putridarium%29_00.jpg.

p. 66. FR Heinrich Maier police photograph. Source: https://www.doew.at/cms/images/5clng/default/1361891801/Maier-Heinrich.png.

Index of Names